Heaven Is Within Us

Fara Gibson

ISBN-10: 1539036979
ISBN-13: 9781539036975

Dedication

This book is dedicated to my Husband, Jim Gibson, The Man in my life whose Soul is intertwined within mine. He supports my journey in Healing the World One Person at a Time without complaint. He makes me feel complete simply by being within my presence. He is the half that makes me whole. He is unconditional love within my life. He has shown me that love doesn't hurt, love isn't jealous, and that love isn't perfect but it is perfect for us. Thank You Jim Gibson, for allowing me to spread my wings in this world without restraint. I Love You More...

I would also like to dedicate this book to those who have allowed me to share the stories of their loved ones who have graduated to Heaven in hopes of helping others in their shoes. I Thank each and Every One of you for sharing your families with me. Thank you for entrusting me to connect you with your loved ones in Heaven. Through your stories of reconnecting with spirit, others have found faith in their greatest time of need. For that, I Thank You and dedicate this book to you.

Most Importantly, I would like to dedicate this book to my family, children, and husband for sharing your time with me, with the world. I know that this path is demanding of me and each of you are so understanding of that part of my journey. With your love and support, this journey is possible. Through your support and love, I am healing others and for that, I am humble and forever grateful.

Table Of Contents

1

Please Allow Me To Introduce Myself

I was going to write this chapter again in a new way, but, when I re-read what I had written in my first book about myself, I thought, well, that about covers it, so why write it again ha ha... So, for those who have read my first book, this may seem familiar and for those of you who purchased this book first, welcome to my journey.

My name is Fara Gibson. I was born in 1977, in Phoenix Arizona. I am a Mother to some amazing children and a Wife to my Soul's Mate Jim Gibson who supports me without question. I am a daughter, a sister, and a friend and even a Grandma. I am also, a Psychic/Medium.

I am asked all of the time, "When did you know that you were a Medium?" The answer to that question is not simple. I was born with the ability to receive messages from Heaven. Over the course of my life, through ups and downs, the ability to communicate with Heaven has always been there. I don't know that I always used it or acknowledged it as a child because I truly didn't understand it. I heard spirit speaking to me, even at a young age. But, I don't think I truly knew, in a world that being a Medium was so Taboo, what it was that was going on within me.

You see, I grew up in a home where life after physical death was not discussed. As a matter of fact, my Dad and I still don't discuss my abilities lol. He says he doesn't believe in psychics or Mediums and I am respectful of that. I will never try to change anyone's mind with their beliefs, and I will never question another's Faith, not even my own Father's. It doesn't mean that my Father loves me any less since we don't share the same beliefs. He supports and loves me in life, and that is what is important.

I can tell you that growing up for me was not easy. I wrote more obstacles into this life that I am living than some people write into 5 lives that they live. I know now, that all of those obstacles that I overcame in life would prepare me for something much bigger in life. I would need the experiences that I learned from in each obstacle in order to empathize with all of the people whose lives I would touch in my future. The obstacles would make me strong enough to stand on my own two feet and take on the world as I set the goal of "Healing the World One Person at a Time", with the support of Heaven. I would have a future filled with people who had many types of obstacles in their lives. If I could relate to all that they had been through, I suppose that would be easier right? Well, it wasn't easy as I went through it by any means lol, but I am thankful for every obstacle in my life as those obstacles have made me into the woman that I am today and I wouldn't change one of them. (Don't get me wrong, I never want to go back and do them again either ha ha)

I began to give specific messages to people here in the physical world from their loved ones in Heaven, in my late teens. I remember watching Television as a teen and seeing Sylvia Browne and John Edwards on their shows or on the Montel Williams Show for Sylvia and I thought to myself, "Whatever Disease it is that John and Sylvia have, is the same Disease that I have!!" They made me feel normal because they were the first I had seen who shared the same ability as I did. But, I had realized that in important times, I was able to give messages that saved lives here. When I did a reading back then, it was not because I had opened a public page and people were reaching out to schedule readings as they are today. Back then, it was a feeling so strong that I needed to give someone a message that I was literally unable to hold myself back from saying what it was to someone that I had to say, no matter what kind of reaction they may have had with me.

I will never forget at a young age, going up to a man whose mother had passed years before. I told him that I had his Mother with me in Spirit. She needed him to know that she was with him at her grave yesterday and she had heard the words that he had said to her. I will keep the rest of what I said private, as it was specific to him. But, when I was finished spouting out all that I had to say to this man, he said to me, "Can I tell you something?" I thought to myself, Oh, please do ha ha (It is pretty awkward at that age to have done something like this). He said, and I will never forget these words. "I was at my Mother's grave yesterday and no one was at the graveyard when I visited her grave. I told her that my marriage was falling apart. I told her that my finances were in shambles. I then told her that I needed to know that she was with me because I was considering SUICIDE, and here you are, the very next day, telling me that you have my Mom with you and she heard me at her grave yesterday." That man is still alive today and is living a life in honor of his Mom to make her proud. How can you put into words, what it feels like to have connected this man with his Mother in Heaven? I can't put it into words, so, I don't even try.

Growing up with this ability was tough for me. I was surrounded by physical abuse from age five to age ten at the hands of a Step Mom, who taught me the lessons of how not to be when I became a Mom myself. I loved to see my first Step Mom go down a divorce path in her life. I always knew that I was filled with love and light. I didn't understand how someone else could choose not to see it themselves. I am now blessed with a beautiful Step Mom who has taken me in as her very own from the moment that she entered my Dad's life.

I went on to be a rebellious teen and I am sure that my spirit Guide George watched most of my teen years thorough his hands over his eyes with a finger cracked for peeking space. In those rebellious stages, at the age of 13, I made one of the worst CHOICES in my life. I took on a relationship out of rebellion because no one liked him. Of course, no one liking him sounded like a pretty good idea to me at the time. But, for 17 years, I paid for that choice by being spit on, told how worthless I was, being punched, and even being choked by the 300 pound man that he was as my children screamed for my life. Through these years, I still had this beautiful ability. I can tell you though, when your life is surrounded by pain and anger, it is hard to see the beauty within yourself. During this time, I still passed messages along to people as spirit made me feel compelled to, but, I was definitely not announcing to the world that I was a Psychic/Medium. I divorced that Man in what was the hardest obstacle that I have ever overcome to this day. I can tell you that it is not an easy decision to make that you will get out, dead or alive, but, either way, at least I would be out.

In the last month of 2008, my whole life changed. I found my Soul's Mate and Love of My Life, Jim Gibson. Jim and I had actually worked together for 10 years prior to realizing that we would be anything more than just technicians that worked for the same phone company. I remember asking myself, "What kind of man takes on a woman and her 4 kids without question and loves them like this?" The answer was simple, it was Jim. Jim showed me what true and unconditional love is. He showed me for the first time in my life, that love does not hurt. Jim made sure that my children and I felt safe from all of the things that had tried to tear me down in my past. I never once played the victim through anything I had been through. I used each and every lesson to make me strong. I would be forever grateful to God for sending Jim Gibson into my life. On May 8th, 2010, at a barbeque that Jim had secretly arranged with my family, Jim dropped down on one knee and asked me to be his wife in front of 50 family members and our children. Of course, I said yes! We were married on December 11th, 2010.

My life didn't just change when I found love with Jim in the form of a relationship together. It also changed my ability to share messages with people much more often than I had ever done growing up. My Grandma said that the reason that I can do what I do now, is because I needed someone like Jim to come into my life and fill it with Unconditional Love, so that I could see all the beauty that was within me. I would say that My Grandma is right. When our focus is in a negative place, painful

4

place, a place of Grief, we tend to miss all of the beauty that is around us and within us. Jim helped me to see how truly beautiful I am. In turn, seeing my own beauty gave me the ability to begin to restore the beauty within each and everyone around me through messages from Heaven.

I suppose that as I introduce myself, I should also introduce my abilities as well. I have never been one to do lots of technical reading on the abilities that I have, so, knowing technical terms and in depth definitions is not my thing lol. Instead, Let me explain it in a way that you will understand it. In my readings, and in speaking with my Spirit Guides, or God, or Jesus, or Angels, It first starts as a feeling that I begin to receive. I would explain this feeling by telling you that I begin to feel LOVE from head to toe that is filled with energy so strong that it will make the hairs stand up on your neck and arms. I feel this energy because I am feeling Heaven. I then begin to gain a knowledge of who it is that is coming through such as Male or Female and young or old or to the side which would be the same age as the client I am speaking to. If it is God, there are no introductions or feelings needed lol as he is so strong and beautiful that there is truly no mistaking his words for another. When I begin to connect with a loved one in heaven, after I establish whether they are male or female and the age range they are in, I begin to ask them questions in my head just as you would think a thought, as this is how I communicate with them back and forth. You see, they do not have bodies in heaven with vocal chords and lungs to create voices. They speak telepathically with one another with no words needed out loud. To hear their voice would be annoying to the ear as it is in such a high pitched frequency that I am grateful that it comes over to me in a thought process. This is the same way that I communicate with them and it goes back and forth in a thought process from me to them and them back to me. As I do this, I have to separate what it is that I am thinking from what it is that they are sending back to me. I will then ask them to tell me how they passed from this life to Heaven. At this point, they will begin to give me indications on my own body as to how they passed. For example, I may have a heavy chest and labored breathing for someone who passed from Lung Cancer and they may give me the thought process of cancer with this to tell me that they were sick with cancer at the end of their life. They may give me a sharp pain in my head and make me point to myself over and over as I pat my chest because I am taking responsibility for taking my life with a gunshot to the head. I may feel as though my right leg has something wrong with it and when I ask the client about their loved one's right leg, they may tell me that it was amputated or had given them trouble in life. I could go on and on with the different passings and indications I receive, but, you get the jest. Once I establish who it is that is coming through and how it is that they passed, they then replace my thoughts, feelings, and emotions with their own. I will see pictures and images within my mind's eye that support what it is that they are trying to say to a loved one. They will give me specific information about themselves or about the loved one that I am speaking to so that they will know without a doubt that this is their loved one in Heaven because no one would have otherwise known that information. I have symbols that I have created within my mind that make it easier for them to tell me things, such as, if they show me a birthday cake with candles, I know that they are trying to acknowledge a birthday. If they show me the Beaches of Normandy, I know they were in WWII and there are many more symbols I have created to make the process for them and I easier in getting their messages across. I had a young male in Heaven make me feel as though I was taking a dip of chew out of my mouth and placing it upon his grave during a reading. His Mom told me that his buddies go to his grave and they each take their chew out of their mouths and place it upon his grave when they visit her son as a gesture of love. You see, I didn't know where to place that information because it truly didn't mean anything to me, but, it meant the world to his Mom to know that her boy sees how his friends honor him even after his passing. Of course, that is just one example. I will include a few reading stories in another chapter to give you a better idea of how my readings go and the information received within them. So, I see pictures and images within my mind's eye, I receive indications within my body to give me more information about their loved one, I hear their thoughts come across over my thought process, and then there is just a knowledge that is unexplainable that comes along with this as well. I suppose that is why they call me a Psychic/Medium. I do get future predictions, medical information, and much more than just communication with Heaven but I always put it like this... I do not make your future or your obstacles in life my focus. Those are the things we are meant to learn and grow from. Your obstacles and future are the reason that you are here on your spiritual journey. I will not hinder the growth of another in this world and I will not make your future predictions my focus. It is a pact that I made with Heaven when I began this journey and I will not break that pact. There are some things that a psychic should ethically keep to themselves and for me, this is one of them. I will not give any negatives as nothing negative comes from heaven. I also get medical indications for people as well from Heaven, but again, I use my Ethics when information about a medical condition for someone comes through. It is not part of my spiritual journey to interfere with someone's path. If I feel that I should recommend blood work or a Dr visit for someone I will, but, I am surely not going to walk up to a stranger and say, "Hey, your liver is shot, sorry".....

I have had a strong team of Angels and Spirit Guides that have supported my journey in life and my communication with them is the same as any other spirit as we do it thorough thoughts and emotions. I just know them as they communicate with me because they have been with me my whole life. When God or Jesus wants their presence to be known in my life, I assure you that they make it beautifully known. I will never forget hearing God's Voice as I began sharing my Abilities with the public. I was driving home from work and I was looking for guidance as to how far I should try to share my abilities with the world. You see, there are many psychic/mediums in this world that never share their abilities or keep them within a close circle. It is not easy to put yourself out there in a world where this ability is still somewhat Taboo. I had to get to a point in my life where I felt as though my Guides and God had given me enough information about Heaven that I could answer any question thrown my way and support any spiritual obstacle that was in front of me. There is Strength in understanding your abilities and I now understood that I could Heal the world one person at a time and

I had set my signs on giving it a good try. It was short and Sweet when God spoke to me as I began this journey and he said, "I Am Sending You Abundance". I remember breaking down in tears as I heard these words as I drove down the street. "Abundance" Do you know what that means? Abundance didn't mean Money or diamond rings and fancy homes. The word "Abundance" stood for the people that God would put in my path for healing. "Abundance" stood for the amount of love and support that God would bless me with as I began to share the Healing that Heaven would offer through me. Through the "Abundance" that God has blessed my path with, I too am Blessed. I Thank God for this Abundance he has blessed me with Every Day...

2

Let's Talk About Heaven Again

I really didn't know where to start on this book, being that it is the second book that I have written. I asked myself if I should repeat some of the information that I placed within the first book just in case someone hasn't had an opportunity to read my first book, "Looking Into The Windows Of Heaven" where I answered so many questions about Heaven. So, I decided to recap some of the important points in that book not only for those who haven't had an opportunity to read it, but as a reminder as well to those who have.

We are all eternal beings who are made of God's pure and unbreakable love, light, and energy. Our souls have lived for an eternity before this life and we will live for an eternity after this life as well. Some of us have lived many lives in our journey (Yes, I have lived more lives than you would like to count). There are also many of you who may be living your very first life as well. We are not made to live lives. Some spirits chose never to live one life at all within their eternity. Our lives are lived for the sole purpose of our Soul's Strength and Growth. You see, Heaven is a place filled with love. Heaven is perfect. Heaven is home for each and every one of us. Because Heaven is so perfect and there is truly not one ounce of negativity within Heaven, we come here to live lives so that our soul may learn and grow from the obstacles that we journey through here on Earth. Some of the obstacles, Love, Addiction, Divorce, Loss, Education, Pain, Illness, financial burden, and the list could go on for an eternity may seem so difficult that we feel we are being given more than we can handle, but, hold your hat when I tell you that God isn't handing you these obstacles… You are……

I feel that each of us plans our own life in its entirety with God, a team of angels to protect us as we live, a spirit guide(or in my case 2 Spirit Guides), as well as with our family members that we will share our lives with before we come to live each life. We work closely with God, our Spirit Guide and with our family to plan the perfect growth that each of us intends to receive in each lifetime that we live. What is a Spirit Guide? A Spirit Guide is someone in Heaven who has lived at least 1 life so that they can empathize with the challenges you are about to experience in life that can't be lived through in the perfect love of Heaven. They are given a copy of your blueprint that you create with God and they are meant to help to guide you for your soul's intended growth as you live. They are that little voice in your head trying to keep you on track, but, they won't interfere as you are given Free Will in life to live and love as you choose. They will give you gentle reminders of your intended path in life and it is up to you and your free will to listen or not. They are not Angels, but, more of a Heavenly Best Friend or sidekick if you will. They still enjoy their amazing comforts of Heaven as they walk at your side and guide you through some of most difficult challenges that you wrote for yourself. They are like a guiding light that you can chose to follow if you will. Your spirit guides are not someone who lived in this life with you, and how could they be, you see, they were assigned to you at Birth. Does that mean that a loved one who passed isn't guiding you? Nope, your loved one who passed can absolutely support your journey in life as well, but, they are not your spirit guide.

Within those lives that we write, we not only write difficult obstacles to work through, but we also give our self Free Will to work through those obstacles in any way that we choose at the time that we go through them. Our choices in how we approach each obstacle can change our paths completely. It is our Free Will that makes those changes in our path and Free Will dictates how amazing or difficult our lives will be as well in many scenarios such as addiction, breaking the law, choosing not to work hard in life, ect..... Overcome these obstacles and you may be destined for Greatness. Let these obstacles overcome you and you may be destined for difficulties, but, in the end, the choice within your growth path is yours. Is there a wrong way to approach each obstacle? NO! There is never a time that you will hear me or God telling you that "You're doing it wrong!" Because, in the end, you are doing it and as you live life, you are growing and learning through each and everything that you live through. There is no right or wrong way, Only "Your Way".

Now that we have our family chosen and our obstacles covered, as we are writing our lives, we also include 5 possible "Exit Points". These are 5 possible times in the life that we will live that we may return to Heaven based upon our soul's growth at the time of each exit. Does God determine when your time to go to will be? Nope.... You do..... I know, this is where your human mind starts screaming, "There is no way my child chose to pass at such a young age!" "There is no way my Husband would have left me like this on his own!". But, sugar coating it for you is truly not my way. I feel that the more we know about life after physical passing, the brighter your healing journey will be. Yes, I am going to tell you that if your loved one did not commit suicide (I will cover that later), then they went in their perfect timing to Heaven. A child that passes at a young age or even at birth is devastating on a human level. The human side of me is impacted by each and every reading that I do when connecting a child in Heaven with their parent here who is grieving with pain beyond description. But, the sprit side of me sees the beauty within that child's passing. I see that the child who passed to Heaven has blessed their family with more growth and strength than they ever knew that they could carry in life. The same can be said for a husband who passed and left behind a beautiful wife in this world to grieve for him. In your Grief, you are gaining strength. Remember when I said, that we write these lives ahead of time, this is where I have to stand on my 2 feet with loving arms wide open telling you how very strong you are for writing such a difficult path in life. I will also tell you that you should be proud of your amazing growth. Then, I need to tell you that you and your family members wrote this path in advance of living it. It is hard to understand with our human mind's I know. But, if you could simply separate your body from your spirit for one moment, Your spirit knew as it planned this life with its loved one, that they would return to be with one another again when each of their human lives are through. As you created this plan, you knew it wouldn't be easy for either of you to walk through this world and work through a tragedy. But, those with the biggest goals of growth will write the most tragic lives. Why? Because life is only temporary and Heaven is eternal. We know this before we come to live a life. We are merely passing through this life for our soul's growth and growing we are surely doing as we work through tragedy. The loved one who passed in that tragedy, on a human level, it is almost impossible to think of all they went through as they passed to heaven. On a spiritual level, their passing becomes quite a cool story to tell in Heaven about how they arrived there, sliding in sideways with their pinky's up in the air screaming Yee Haw! Perhaps a loved one will take their first possible exit as an infant and in that passing, they bless their family with love and strength that they never knew that they could carry as well as more love than they ever knew they could hold. Maybe a loved one takes a passing in the middle of their exit options as a late teen or young adult. We look at these passings of youngsters as tragic. I say, "How Beautiful are they to have reached their Amazing Soul's Growth in such a small amount of time?" Maybe a loved one lives a long life and takes the 5th exit in their plan. Perhaps their life was meant to support the lives of others for a length of time and they did just that until they were the amazing age of 80 to 100 years old.

What I want you to do now, is look around you. No one is in your life by chance. Everyone in your life, even the stranger you meet on the street has an impact upon your path in life. Perhaps you can look around you and pick out the people in your life that are meant to be lessons for you. I know that I could name a few family members and people in my past that were meant to be lessons for me. You know, those difficult ones that you just wish would be shipped off to an island somewhere and be eaten by fire ants? Okay, maybe not fire ants, but at least a few swarms of bees on that island would be nice ha ha.... Okay, you get my jest. I want you to look at all of those people who are difficult in your life and quietly in your mind, I want you to say, "Thank You". What??!! Did she just tell us to thank all of those Idiots??!! Yep, you see, those people who have been most difficult in your life, have also blessed you with more strength and growth than any other person in this world could. I know it wasn't easy living through it, but carrying anger for them is not serving you. I want you to replace that anger with a big, "Thank You". "Thank you for making me the person that I am today, because that person is pretty dang amazing and without the lessons of Jerks like you in my life, I wouldn't be this strong!" Now, letting that anger go, feels pretty good doesn't it. You see, if you carry that anger, you are allowing their lessons to take hold of you. The anger will weigh you down. The anger will start manifesting in your body with health conditions. The anger will make you lose sleep. Then anger will define you because it is your focus and what you place your focus on in life brings about more of the same. Carrying that anger will push everyone away that is trying to surround you with love and you will begin to feel you are walking through the world alone. It isn't easy to be a loving soul trying to comfort someone who emanates pain and anger and so many times, they must move to seclude themselves from you as they honor their own worth. So, a simple Thank You keeps intact the beautiful person you are and doesn't give any more of your beauty to that situation from this day forward. Let them be as ugly in this world as they would like. We will thank them from afar for being lessons for others in their growth path as well.

Now that you have lived your life and grown through your journey of paths in life, what happens when you pass to Heaven? What happened to your loved ones when they passed to Heaven?

When you pass to Heaven, you are instantly filled with God's Pure Love. When we pass to Heaven, we all become the age of 30. I have asked my Spirit Guides, why is everyone 30 when they pass and they simply answer me with, Why Not? I suppose that when I look at the age of 30, it is an age where we began to reach maturity in life without feeling old. So, the old become young and vibrant again when they pass and the young become older, wiser, and we can view them as more self sufficient when they pass rather than worry about an infant or child that needs care in Heaven. Does that take away from them being your child in life? No, but you see, they were an eternal soul long before they became your child in this life and they have simply returned to their soul's place in Heaven. Not to worry Mama, you will know your child and the bond that you have with one another in Heaven. When we pass to Heaven, we are instantly surrounded by all of our loved ones who passed before us. We instantly have a full memory and knowledge of Heaven and who those loved ones were for us in this life as well as in our Eternity before we lived this life. When we pass to Heaven, we are instantly filled with more love and peace than I could ever put into words for you. Life's troubles such as pain, anger, arguments, finances, illness and any other negative thought feeling or emotion that you could think of simply disappear when you pass to Heaven. No matter the way that we pass, the outcome of peace and comfort in Heaven is still the same. Murder victims don't wait for revenge before they are at peace. Babies that pass don't need to wait for their Mommies before they carry on to God's pure light. Someone who passed in a vehicle accident does not remain at the accident site for all eternity when they pass. A loved one that passed from an illness does not carry that illness to Heaven. When I say that they are filled with peace and love, I want you to know that they don't even miss you in Heaven. Missing you would be a negative emotion and they are simply not capable of feeling negative emotions in Heaven. So, instead of missing you from Heaven, they Love you from Heaven.

As they arrive in Heaven, they begin a life review. They will re-live their life through the eyes of everyone that they ever touched with their life. They will live their life through the eyes of parents, siblings, teachers, aunts, uncles, friends, foes, spouses, exes, co-workers, and more types of relationships that I could begin to list here, yes even strangers on the street that they simply passed by. When I say that they live their life through the eyes of everyone their life ever touched, I meant

EVERYONE. They will see how much they were loved. They will see how much love that they made an effort to share with others in this world as well. They may see how they could have placed more effort on sharing that love within this world and that becomes a lesson of love for them in Heaven. Perhaps they had an addiction in life that they overcame and they will find a sense of pride and growth for overcoming such a difficult obstacle in life. Perhaps that addiction carried through their life into their passing and they will see all of the strength it took for them to continue such a difficult path in life as they grew through that addiction and they will know how much that addiction affected their family and loved ones in life as well. They will see how their hard work in life impacted the lives of others. They may have moments that they are not proud of at all, but even those moments carry lessons of growth. You see, some people may refer to these lessons as sin or mistakes and I see them as a beautiful spirit learning and growing through life just as they intended. Who are we to judge the path of another? If they aren't on a path that we agree with, we always have the Free Will to take a step back from them. Do you think that in your life review that you will be upset with yourself for taking a step back from someone on a negative path and honoring your worth? I can tell you, if you took that step back, you just overcame one of your most difficult obstacles in life as well just as you intended and you will be proud of that. It doesn't mean that you love someone any less when you take that step back. But, it does mean that they are always welcome to join you on your positive path in life someday when they are ready, if that day comes for them, but in the mean time, you are honoring your worth and your strength as well.

As we re-join our Heavenly Home, we already have a space awaiting us that has been there all along while we lived our life. Oh yes, our home in Heaven is still there... Perhaps that "dream home" you have always wanted is truly a dream because it is already yours in Heaven. You see, I have to ask you again to separate your mind from body and spirit. Our souls have had a home in Heaven for an Eternity before we came here to live a life and when we pass to Heaven, we simply return Home. We don't have to build a house and make new friends, and search endlessly for a family member so that we won't feel lonely. Nope, you need not worry about them as they are in perfect peace. They no longer have bodies to hold them back. Your loved ones soar through the air with ease in Heaven, no, we don't have wings in Heaven, Angels have wings, but, WE DO FLY! You may have felt the sensation of flying in a dream in life and that is your soul simply traveling outside of your body as your body rests, and it wasn't really a dream at all, but instead astral travel where your spirit leaves your body as you sleep.

As your loved ones arrive in Heaven, they are surrounded by those who love them. Eternal relationships pick up just as they left off before we came to live a life. They are reunited with their Spirit Guides whom guided them through some of the most difficult challenges in life. And then, there is you. Yes, you are still living and they are very aware of that. They watch you as you live. They don't miss one milestone in your life. They hear you speak to them both silently in your mind as well as out loud. They see the ways that you honor them after their passing and I can assure you that no matter how much or how little you spend in honoring them, it is simply the gesture of love that you share in honoring them that means the most to them. They see you stumble in life. They find pride in your living for they lived a life themselves and they realize that living is not an easy thing to do.

People often ask me what kind of time frame exists between us living lives. That question is honestly impossible for me to answer. The reason for it being impossible to answer is there is no sense of time in Heaven. Heaven is Eternal and so how do you place a time on Eternity? We as humans created time. We needed time to keep track of our age, when we needed to go to school, when we needed to get to work, when we were done working, when to arrive at a party, when to be present for a funeral, but time is not something we need in Heaven. Some loved ones in Heaven may only live one life and this life they shared with you was the only life they will ever live. Some loved ones have goals for 5 more lives and perhaps they begin to work on the blue print for their next life from the moment that they arrive back in Heaven. Does that mean that they won't be there for you when you return to Heaven? No, it doesn't mean that at all. You see, in a place where time is eternal, there is no rush to plan the next life. Each life is carefully calculated for their growth and their intentions of providing growth for others as well. I find that if they do return into another life while you are still living that you will know without a doubt in your soul that they have returned. Perhaps they come back into your family as a grandchild or perhaps a niece or nephew, maybe even as your very own child. But, your soul will recognize theirs and it will be unmistakable. Many lives lived have about 100 years or more difference when speaking in our length of time. 98% of your loved ones will be awaiting you when you arrive in Heaven. Perhaps a Great Grandfather has returned and you find this out when you arrive in Heaven. Please don't go through life wondering if they will be there, for when your soul returns to Heaven, you will have a clear and peaceful knowledge of Heaven and your loved ones who reside there with you.

But, what about Hell? Do our loved ones that "Sinned" go to Hell? Will I ever see them again? I get asked this question quite often and I may turn your world upside down right now when I tell you that there is no such thing as Hell. Let me explain to you in my best short version in this recap, my perspective through Heaven's eyes on Hell. Yes, I know that there is an amazing book called The Bible that speaks of a place called Hell. But, I want you to take a step back from that book for a moment. The Bible was written by man many years ago. The Bible was written by man who could hear Heaven. Within that Bible is love, peace, and understanding that I feel is absolutely the word of God. Also, within the pages of the Bible is the Ego of Man. What do I mean by that? Well, man who interpreted the Bible could hear God and Heaven right? My question here is what makes me and any other true Mediums any different from that Man as we hear Heaven as well. But, what happens when I or anyone else that hears Heaven relays the messages to others that we receive? These messages are left open to our interpretation of how they are coming across to us. Within that interpretation, there is always room for human error and the other thing there is room for is human Ego. Ego is the one thing written into the Bible that I don't agree with. You see, as many years ago at the Bible was written t here was a great need for control in this world. What better way to control in this world than by leading with fear. Do this, or else? Listen to me, or else? Do only as I say, I mean as God says, or else? But, what would the "Or Else" be? Why not create a horrible place where a monster lives (The Devil), where people burn and are tortured for all eternity if they don't listen to me and my perspective? Then, people will listen!!! There is even a passage or two in the Bible that say that you should never listen to a Medium or Psychic. Well, how on Earth would he rule by fear if you heard the love and peace of Heaven coming from another Medium and you actually listened to them? And so, I feel that Man created Hell as a way to imprint his views and beliefs upon others in a way that made them listen. I feel that you should take every judgmental and negative word that is within the pages of the Bible and remove them. When you have removed the negativity within the pages of the Bible, it is then that you are listening to the Love of God. God is all loving and completely unconditional. God does not judge your life that you live. You are living this life for your very own growth for your spirit. Why on Earth would God punish you for stumbling and falling in life where you are meant to for your growth? The answer to that question is that God wouldn't punish you at all. Remember when I said that you go into a life review when you arrive in Heaven? I didn't say that God reviews your life. God already walked through your life with you and he has no need to review it. Did you reach your growth that you had intended to achieve in this life that you lived? If so, you will be proud of your growth. If you didn't achieve your growth that you intended, then perhaps you will decide to live another life to continue that growth for yourself. This place that we live in is as close to "Hell" that you will ever be. The world we live in is filled with negativity and within our paths in life, we are to find love in a place that is so negative and that is not easy. God is proud of you, for you are living and he knows that living is not easy to do. But, if there is no Hell, then what happens to "Bad" people? That is a broad question and I am going to answer both ends of the spectrum on that question. What you may interpret as "Bad" is your judgment and perhaps that "Bad" person was simply living out a contract that they made long before they came to live this life with the person that they were "Bad" to. You see, if life were easy, what would we learn from it? So, there are spirits that come here to live a life who are meant to provide challenges in the lives of others. On a human level, we would like them to be shipped off to an island full of bees and left there for all eternity for the miserable turmoil they have caused in our paths or in the paths of a loved one. On a spiritual level, I can tell you that they will rejoin one another in Heaven with a big huge high 5 at a job well done. Oh yes, they may have "Hated" one another in life, done unspeakable things to each other, but within those obstacles that they overcame with one another lies the strength and growth that our souls came here for in the first place. I am going to get as specific as saying that not every murder is some malicious intent from a monster who is living on this Earth. Most times, murders that are random as planned with the victim and the murderer long before they come here to live. The victim would have wanted to pass in such a way that they arrive in Heaven with ultimate growth through their passing and a pretty cool story to tell in Heaven about how they arrived. The murderer would have wanted to experience what it is to take a life, and live within a life of say prison, and all of the consequences that come along with making the decision to take a life in this world. These are not things we have the ability to experience in Heaven that is so perfect and within these difficult lessons lies the most growth for our souls. Then, there are those that life with malicious intent to hurt others in this world. These souls have completely turned away from the light of God and any form of love in this world that surrounds them. They have stopped living their life as their blueprint intended and hurt and kill others that was not within their plan. Yes, I do believe that there are negative souls in this world and so, what happens to them when they pass if there is no such thing as Hell? They go right back into living another life immediately when they pass. There is no beautiful layover in Heaven with the choice to continue their soul's growth as we have. They don't get to rejoin the comfort and peace of God's pure love and light with their family and friends in Heaven. They go straight back into utero to do it again and again and again until they begin to find love in their life in some form once again.

But, what if we don't find God or Religion in life? Does that make me or my loved one bad? I don't feel that we have to find God or religion in life for we are a part of God. God removes all memories we have of him and of Heaven before we come to live this life because life would be so much easier if we had a full memory of Heaven. Why on Earth would God punish us in a world where our memories of him were stripped away simply because we didn't find him here? The God I know doesn't punish us at all. What would the challenge in life be, if we had a full memory of the beautiful place we will return to that is perfect in every way. You aren't going to be punished because you didn't find religion in this life. Perhaps part of your path was trying to live in this life without a knowledge of God at all (Since you know him so well at home) and working through the struggles of living a life without the belief that there is so much more to life than this.

There was much more in my first book than what I summed up in this chapter. But, if you hadn't had an opportunity to read my previous book, this chapter will give you a better understanding of where I am taking you next. I hope to answer questions in this book that I hadn't answered in the previous book. May it give you a new outlook on the beauty that surrounds you in this world.

3

Are They Happy Now In Heaven?

One of the most commonly questions asked of me by people who have a loved one in Heaven is, "Are they happy now in Heaven?" The simple answer to this question is, "Yes". But, now I would like to help you to understand the words "Yes, they are Happy", in a way that will resonate within your soul.

I suppose that before I can tell you that they are happy, we need to discuss the reasons they were unhappy here on Earth in their lifetime to begin with.

People are unhappy here on Earth for many reasons. Why is it that they are unhappy in life? Well, It's Earth, which is the opposite of Disney Land and it is one of the unhappiest places to put it nicely. You see, we come from Heaven to live this life on Earth so that we may learn from our difficult or "unhappy" times. When we are in Heaven, we are in a place of pure and unconditional love. In Heaven, we are free of pain, sadness, worry, fear, anger, jealousy, and any negative thought, feeling, or emotion you could ever imagine here on Earth. We are surrounded by peace and understanding in Heaven. We are comforted by God's pure and amazing light in all that we do in Heaven. When we come to live here on Earth, all of the peace and unconditional love that we once knew in Heaven is removed from our memory. Upon arrival in our new little body at birth, we are born into a place of pain and discomfort compared to where we just came from in Heaven. We begin to feel emotions during our birth that we have never felt before in heaven. As an infant, the simple discomfort of hunger is nothing like anything we ever felt when we were in Heaven because in Heaven we don't have a need to eat. Let's face it, we didn't have these awkward bodies in Heaven that make crazy noises, stink, feel pain, feel fear, and could grow a random zit in a day and that in itself could take some getting used to and make an individual a bit perturbed.

One common thread with each of us who are born into living a life on Earth, is the opportunity for Learning and Growth in each of our paths. But, where do we learn and grow here on Earth? The answer to this question is simple. Your Strength comes from your struggles. Your knowledge comes from your trials. For, if life were easy, then what would you learn from it? Besides, if life were meant to be perfect and easy, then we would have no need to leave Heaven.

There are too many obstacles to list that we grow from in life, but some of the common ones are; Love, Divorce, Education, Arguments, Substance Addiction, Long term and short term Illness, Disabilities, Family Trouble, Finances, Work, Loss of A Loved One, and I am sure that I could go on forever listing our life obstacles. But, without these obstacles in our lives, where would we be? Who would we be? These obstacles are not intended to defeat us. The obstacles in our path are intended to make us stronger as we journey through life. Someday, when we reach the end of this lifetime, we will look back upon all of the obstacles that we made it through and realize that within those hard times, we found greatness.

But, sometimes, the obstacles that we are faced with in life can feel like a train running us over. We can feel helpless to the obstacle when we forget our strength. We can feel defeated by the obstacle when we don't remind ourselves of our beauty. We may have family disagreements over an obstacle which in turn makes the obstacle feel even more out of reach to overcome. What we may forget on this journey from time to time, is that we have the ability to make it through anything that life throws our way with flying colors. But, there we are, Unhappy in life.... Unhappy because we have taken an addiction we can't seem to kick? Unhappy because we need a divorce but we haven't found the strength to honor our worth and so we stay? Unhappy because we can't get on top of our finances? Unhappy because we have a terminal illness and we just simply don't feel good? Unhappy because our close loved one passed and we miss their physical presence terribly? We are unhappy because we simply get caught up in life.

I have heard it said by many people, "Earth is Hell". I have to say that I agree because this Earth thing is as bad as it gets folks. Your trials, obstacles, or whatever you'd like to call them are the most difficult things your soul will ever have to endure for its own growth. The crazy thing to wrap your head around when it comes to these "Obstacles" is that we wrote them into our lives ourselves for our very own growth. Wait!! What??!!! Yes, I said that you wrote these obstacles and so did your loved one who is in Heaven. I know, this is the part where your human mind says, "Look Lady, there is no way possible that I or my loved one wrote this into our life on purpose!" This is also the part where I stand my ground and say, yes, you and they did. If you take all of your human self into your hand and please set it aside for a moment that would be great. Okay, now it is your soul and I speaking. Your soul knows that these struggles are where its strength comes from. Some of the Strongest Souls write some of the most difficult lives! Now, I want you to look back on all of the difficulties you have made it through with a 100% track record of making it through them, and I want you to be proud of yourself. What did you learn from your path in life? Who are you because of the obstacles in your path? Who was your loved one in life because of their obstacles? What did they learn from their obstacles?

Now we are going to get to the question at the top of this chapter, "Are They Happy?" YES! They are 100% without a doubt Happy in Heaven. Those obstacles that they wrote for themselves that made them unhappy were for their soul's growth and growing they did! Those difficult times

FARA GIBSON

that seemed to defeat them in life have now become strengths for them in Heaven because of the knowledge gained in those difficult times.

Perhaps the thought of how they passed to Heaven, leaves you with the question of if they are happy now because it was a painful passing, or sudden passing, or tragic passing? I want you to look at those passings differently after today. I want to give you my prison analogy for this explanation not because your loved ones are by any means in prison, but it is one of the easiest ways for me to explain this. People arrive in Heaven many different ways much like how people arrive in prison. You see the movies, right? You know, when the new prisoner walks in to the cell and all the other guys that are already sitting in the cell before them say, "Hey Man, What you in for?" Then the new inmate proceeds to tell the other inmates the story of how they arrived..... Some of them are there on simple charges like an argument that got a little heated and some may be there for having marijuana in their car, while others are there for some of the big reasons that make the other guys all go "OOOHHHH!" I say that our arrival in Heaven or the HOW we get there is much the same. Our loved ones and friends who are in Heaven are there before us just waiting to embrace us when we arrive. As we get there or HOW we get there is our story and part of our legacy. You look at a tragedy as devastating and that is because you are Human and fueled by Love or the search for Love in this place that it is so difficult to find and tragic passings of our loved ones are devastating because they are unexpected and they are well, tragic! For a loved one or Sprit, to have passed by tragedy, it becomes a cool story when they reach Heaven. Upon arrival after their tragedy, I always picture these spirits Sliding into Heaven sideways with their Pinky's Up in the air screaming "WOOO HOOOO WHAT A RIDE!!!" All of their loved ones and friends in Heaven gather around for the story of how they arrived in Heaven and there are many there who passed from cancer, or illness, or passed in their sleep. (Not that anyone's passing is better or worse than anyone else because there truly is no competition between us in Heaven either as it is our own growth we are after and we encourage the growth of others) But, you see, a loved one that passed in a rollover accident here on Earth is a tragedy for us.

24

When they get to Heaven and tell of that rollover accident, it is like a Bull Rider describing his 8 second ride!!!! It is an exciting story for them to tell as they arrive in Heaven and in that passing there were lessons learned. Their story and those lessons will make perfect sense to them as they arrive HAPPILY in Heaven. Those of us left behind tend to focus on the thought of them feeling pain when they passed, or suffering in that passing. When our loved one arrives in Heaven, there is no pain and all of the memories of how they got there become part of their growth. How on Earth could their intended passing with such a cool story upon arrival in Heaven make them sad? It doesn't. It just makes us sad because we are still living here on Earth where all of our memories of living life in pure happiness have been removed and the only thing we can possibly focus on is the tragedy. So, in focusing on the tragedy, we begin to think of our loved ones as being as miserable as they must have been in the moment that they passed or as miserable as we are? But, I can assure you that is your conscious human mind creating scenarios out of your focus that only punish you.

Once your loved one arrives in Heaven, every single ounce of pain, anger, suffering, or negative thought, feeling, or emotion, is completely removed from their soul. They don't carry grudges with them to Heaven. They aren't angry that a loved one had to make a decision to take them off of life support. They don't stress about the financial debt they had in life. They don't ask around upon arrival in Heaven for the local Heroin dealer. They don't worry about physical abuse. They move to a place made of complete love. There are NO EXCEPTIONS to this Statement, THEY ARE MADE OF GOD'S PURE AND AMAZING LIGHT AND THEY ARE HAPPY.

It doesn't make your loved one in Heaven unhappy to see you unhappy. There is no possible way that you could disappoint them in Heaven. They lived a life as well and they know the struggle of working through pain in life. Instead of asking "Is my loved one disappointed because I cry all the time for them?" Why not focus on doing something in honor of your loved one so that those tears may be turned into a smile, if only for a moment. They aren't disappointed in you for a moment and instead, they encourage your smile. They don't sit in Heaven crying with you, heck they don't even miss you! I don't say that to be mean, I say that because negative emotions don't exist in Heaven and what kind of Heaven would Heaven be if we all got there and desperately missed everyone we love?! When we arrive in Heaven, we can see our loved ones as they are living their life still. We don't miss out on even the smallest details of their life as we watch over our family from Heaven. We cheer them on in their successes. We see their new relationships. We hold their babies first in Heaven as we hand them down to our loved ones. We attend the weddings of our loved ones in life. We hear their thoughts and words to us always. We can enjoy the beauty and peace of Heaven and still walk at the side of our loved ones who are still living a life at the same time without missing a beat.

You see, the only person unhappy between you and your loved one in Heaven, is you. So, what can you do to find happiness again after the passing of a loved one? Well, I can tell you that Happiness is not something that is going to creep back into your life. You will not wake up one day and suddenly you find that your life is so perfect that you find yourself skipping through a parking lot singing Zippety Doo Dah. Happiness is created, it is worked for, it is made. You have the ability within you to create happiness. This is where you tell me that you are so depressed and devastated that there is no way you can be happy again. I say that as long as that is your focus, you may be right. My question is, are you happy being depressed and devastated? Or, do you miss the person that you once were before the tragedy? The choice is yours. Which choice will you be proud of when you look back on these moments?

Let me give you a few choices. You can stay in bed or inside your home and cry all day. You can push the ones you love away from you with your negativity as they try to give you love and then complain that no one is around you to support you anymore. You can hold on to the day and memory of the way a loved one passed and let that be the legacy of their whole life left behind for you. Or. You can wake up in the morning and as your feet hit the floor you can invite your loved one in Heaven to walk this day with you. You can do 1 thing however small each day that honors the legacy of love that your loved one left behind. As the memories of your loved one's passing creep into your mind, you can consciously remove those thought and replace those thoughts with a fond memory of your loved one or perhaps even speak to them in that moment as a distraction as you tell yourself, "The way that they passed is not my focus as my focus is upon how they Lived and Loved in this world". You can decide that every time you get out of your car in a parking lot that you will sing Zippety Doo Dah in honor of your loved one in Heaven all the way from your car to the door of the establishment that you have arrived at while you skip with every step. Do you think that is crazy? I do it all of the time. I even taught my kids to do it as well ha ha. Why? Because it honors my smile and it creates smiles for those around us that are looking on. Because, in that wacky moment, there is love, humor, spontaneity, and a statement that today is a "Wonderful Day". Try it and see how many people smile at you, perhaps they needed that smile more than you will ever know. (They may be laughing at you and not with you, but I always say, Hey, live life to it's fullest no matter what others may think)

So, "Are They Happy?" My answer to that question is yes. Are you Happy? If you answered yes, then carry on with your smile. If your answer is no, what choices can you make in your life to make a difference in that statement. Remember, here on Earth, Happiness does not just come to us, it is created.

4

The More You Know, The Less You'll Hurt

There isn't one thing that I could say that would ease your pain that you carry because the physical presence of your loved one who has graduated to Heaven is no longer here. You miss their smile, their touch, their physical presence of love. You miss what could have been within your future with them. You may miss the opportunities you had when they were here that you didn't take with them. I'm sure I couldn't begin to list all of the things that you miss about your loved ones in Heaven. I can't help that you miss those things; because your life here as you know it is forever changed by their passing.

What I can help you with is knowledge, understanding, and recognition to help you on your grieving path. You see, your loved one that joined you on this journey in life is a soul that your soul has known for an eternity before this lifetime. You and your loved one have spent more "Time" together in that Eternity than you could even begin to fathom. Your bond with one another is bright, strong, and unbreakable. There isn't a soul in this universe that could separate your bond of love with one another. That bond can also never be broken simply by one of you graduating to Heaven before the other in life. You will know this love that you share in life long after your physical life is through. Actually, the love that you know in the life after this with them is much stronger than you could ever begin to imagine. If you take all of the love you have felt for one another and multiply it by infinity, you may begin to understand the strength of love in Heaven.

You and your loved one wrote this life together long before you came here to live it. Because there are so many different scenarios of relationships you may have had with one another, Parent and Child, Husband and Wife, Siblings, Friends, I truly won't be able to touch upon each individual journey, but what I can touch on is Spirit. Your spirits came to live this life for the amazing growth that you intended for your souls. There is a saying, "If life were easy, what would we learn from it?" That saying couldn't be more true for each of us. You see, we already come from a place that is perfect. There are no negative thoughts, feelings, or emotions in Heaven. There is no pain or anger or struggle as we live in God's pure light in Heaven. If we wanted to continue to bask in that amazing light and stay in Heaven, the choice is ours to do so. Many spirits never incarnate to live even one life, let alone many. Then there are those of us who have an insatiable yearning for growth and learning. We plan these lives in a place where the love and memory of Heaven is stripped from us upon arrival and it is up to us to find that love in this difficult world through our journeys. You will have highs in your path and unmistakable lows as well along your way. There will be moments you wish you could live again because you aren't proud of them. There will be moments you long to live again because they felt so amazing. But, in your journeys, there will also be tragedy. Why tragedy? Because tragedy is impossible in Heaven. It is the one thing that you grow more from than anything else in this universe. Tragedy brings more strength into your path that you ever dreamed that you could carry. "Wait??!! I am supposed to live through this crap??!!" Not only are you living through it intentionally, you planned it with your family long before this journey began. I know that statement just made some of you angry at me, but the only thing that I can be in educating you so that you have a better understanding, is HONEST. I can sugar coat it like most people would, but as I began this journey, I decided that enough people sugar coat things and the only way to truly heal someone is through honesty. I know you look at the tragedy of your loss of your loved one as the most devastating thing you have even fathomed going through and you are right, it is. Whether it was an illness, suicide, accident, murder, the outcome is still the same and not one of these passings is any more or less important than the other. For us, it becomes a devastating story of how our life is forever changed by the passing of a loved one. I can tell you that in Heaven, there is a completely different side to their passings. I want you to take a step outside of your human body for a moment and join me in spirit. Now, look at yourself with me for just a moment if you will. Before your loved one passed, life was amazing, or at least more amazing than when they passed on a human level. Things were different when they were still here, as your days were filled with their love and the peace of having them at your side. Now, I want to remind you that you have that love and peace in Heaven. I want you to be extremely proud of yourself for finding those feelings of love and peace here on Earth because as I said before, that is not easy to do in a world that is full of so much negativity that our spirits have never experienced before. I want you to look at their passing with me from a place of spirit as well. You see, their passing has blessed your path with more strength and love than you ever knew it was possible to carry in this world. THAT strength and love is a Gift that they left for you in this world before they journey'd home to Heaven. I know that when you step back into your human body in a moment that Strength and Love will feel like a burden again, so heavy that you aren't sure you can carry it. When it gets to be so heavy, I want you to take a step back to spirit for a moment again and allow yourself to feel pride for the strength you are receiving in this world. Not everyone writes paths that are so difficult and you should be in awe of your very own strength, because, I can tell you that I am. When your loved one arrives in heaven, that tragic event that brought about their passing becomes such a cool story of how they arrived in Heaven. It is the essence of them and part of the legacy they left behind. I know that when we look at it from our human eyes, we don't see anything cool about it at all. But, you must remember that no matter what these human bodies endure in this life time, our SPIRITS ARE ALWAYS UNTOUCHED as our spirits are made of God's pure love and light and that is unbreakable. I use the analogy at times to make it more understandable that when we arrive in Heaven, it is much like when convicts are sitting around in a jail cell saying "How'd you get here man?". I like to picture our loved ones sliding into Heaven sideways sometimes with their pinkys up in the air screaming Yeee Hawwww as they arrive with their cool stories to tell. Some of them have stories of how they battled cancer. Others may arrive with a story of being murdered with all of the details that make the other spirits around them drop their spiritual jaws. Some may have lived short lives in which they lived those lives to bless their family with strength through their passing. Some may have lived long lives and passed mid step in their home before they arrived in Heaven with their story. Whatever their story, it is theirs and you are blessed that they shared part of that life story with you. If you were there for a tragedy, I want you to know that in their passing, their spirit couldn't have imagined anyone more amazing to spend their final moments with than you. You see, I see blessings in even the most difficult situations when I look through the eyes of spirit. If you were not there when a loved one passed, it is because they did it in their own way and you are meant to remember them for how they lived in this life. So, if you are carrying guilt for not being there, simply put it down. You would have been there if you could have and they know that.

When your loved one passes, they move back into the perfect and amazing light if God in Heaven. They are instantly filled with love as they rejoin family and friends that they met in this lifetime and long before this lifetime as well. They see you from Heaven for Heaven is all around you here on Earth. Heaven is only 3 feet off of our floor. Yes, 3 feet. So, look down where your feet are and go up 3 feet from there and that is where our loved ones feet walk, or glide, in Heaven. It is why when someone says that they saw their Mom in spirit and she floated into the room.... Mom wasn't floating above our floor, she was walking on hers. Because heaven is so close to us, they see us from Heaven. They hear your words and your silent thoughts to them as well. They see how you honor them. They comfort you when you cry. They encourage you to live life to it's fullest as they are right here at your side. People often ask me if they are happy in Heaven? I say that it is us that aren't happy because of all that we have endured in this life, but They Are Happy in Heaven.

I hope this has brought some peace and comfort into your day. I pray it has answered some of your difficult questions when it comes to the "Loss" of a loved one. You see, I will never use the word "Died" or "Dead", because though their bodies couldn't carry in in this physical life, their spirits are Eternal and never for a moment "Died". Carry them with you in all that you do. Look for the amazing signs that they surround you with from Heaven. Know that when you see those signs and your thoughts go to your loved ones in Heaven that those signs are truly from them and don't let your conscious mind tell you any different. Your loved ones are limitless when it comes to sending those signs. Have faith that this will all make perfect sense some day. May your joys be fulfilled, your dreams be blessed by visits with your loved ones in Heaven, and your strength help you to reach heights you never knew you could reach in life.

5

Ghosts Or Spirits In Your Home?

I have had a lot of people reaching out to me out of fear of spirit or ghost activity in their home. I wanted to touch on this subject a little bit because it is something that is very common since spirit is all around us.

As we begin this conversation, I want you to please take everything that you've ever learned in a scary movie right now and throw it out the window. Just take all of your visions of Freddy Krueger and Michael Myers and Cousin It LOL and wad them up in a ball and throw them right out the window. Okay perfect, now, all that you should have left in your beautiful brain is proof of spirit or ghosts.

Some people look at Spirit or ghost from a place of fear. I look at Spirit and ghosts as beautiful proof that there is so much more to life than our physical presence here on Earth.

Since Heaven is here on Earth just three feet above our floor, it is very common for us to sense a spirit around us. We may feel as though our loved ones who have passed to Heaven are near us at times and that is because they are. We may have visual sightings of our loved ones who have passed and please know that those sightings are very real because they are all around you. You may simply get signs from a loved one letting you know that they are around. Perhaps they manipulate your electronics in your home or move items. Maybe they simply send birds or butterflies around you. But whatever the signs they give it is because your loved ones and spirit are truly trying to let you know that Heaven is all around you and that they are okay and loving you and watching over you and hearing you from heaven.

But, what about when you walk into a room and you get a really uneasy feeling? The hairs on the back of your neck stand up and you feel as though there's a ghost in the room but, the ghost definitely doesn't want you there. You're probably right and they probably are there and they probably don't want you there and here is the reason why. When a ghost is grounded here on Earth, they see things in their surroundings in the way that they were at the time of their passing. So, perhaps you have a new home and you don't understand why you have a ghost because it's new, but you see that land that your new house is on was there long before you and perhaps so are they. Maybe you brought an antique in the home that was theirs in life that they particularly like and they have come with the antique. This would still give them a view of your home as if it was theirs in the way that it was before they passed. You see, to them, you are an intruder into their space. I always use this analogy when explaining this. I am a mom and I have children and if someone were to break into my home, I would want The Intruders to get out as well just as a ghost wants you out of their space. They don't understand who you are or why you are in their space, but they do understand that it is their space. So, you may catch an electronic voice phenomenon on a digital recorder that says "Get Out." People get really scared by this and I have to giggle a little inside when I hear of this because I would say the same thing if someone that I didn't know were to walk into my home. Maybe they cause a ruckus and move things and try to scare you but wouldn't you do the same thing if someone were in your home?

People then say to me well, how can I get rid of a ghost? My best suggestion for getting rid of a ghost is telling them about heaven. You see, most ghosts don't understand that they have passed. Sometimes it's best to start there in a conversation with them. Wait?! Did I say that we were going to have a conversation with a ghost?! I sure did! You see at one time they were human and living a very Human Experience just like you and I. For whatever their personal reasons were, they didn't cross over to heaven. It doesn't make them all bad. Sometimes they simply wanted to wait for a loved one but they don't realize that in there waiting, they've lost all track of time and their loved one may already be in heaven before them. Perhaps they did some things in life they weren't so proud of and they were afraid of facing God when they passed and so they decided to stay here grounded as a ghost. What they didn't understand is God doesn't judge them when they get to heaven. We are our own worst critics of Our Lives when we get to heaven. Those things that they called mistakes that they made in life were simply lessons that they were meant to learn and grow from in spirit. But, whatever the reason that they stayed behind and are grounded here as a ghost, the fact is, we can help them.

If you have a ghost in your home that seems to be a bit of a pest, my suggestion is to sit down in that room and have an out loud conversation with them. Introduce yourself first and tell them who you are. Perhaps nicely letting them know that this is your home or space that they are residing in is a good start. The next thing you will need to tell them is that they have passed and that their body is no longer living although their Spirit lives. I typically remind them that they had many loved ones and friends here on Earth at the time that they lived and many of them may now be in heaven waiting for them. At this point I tell them, please look up above you and you will see a beautiful white light coming down above your head. If you go to that beautiful light, your loved ones will be waiting there for you. God will be there to embrace you as well without judgment. All of your friends and family will embrace you as you arrive and you will be in a place of pure love and peace. It is typically at this point that I feel the room lightens as I feel them exit and go to heaven. Of course the choice is theirs because we truly can't make them go. But I've never run into a ghost that I couldn't talk over to heaven because what they want more than anything is your help to find heaven, peace, and love and they just don't know it. What could possibly be scary about that?

People often ask me if a ghost can harm them. My answer to that is always no. I know, there's a whole bunch of ghost chasing shows out there on TV and somebody got scratched LOL. If you look at the surroundings that these guys are traipsing around in in the dark, it isn't any wonder that someone got a little scratch or two or three. They walk around provoking trying to get that perfect shot on video and of course I have to giggle again because if I'm that ghost and some jerk is provoking me I'm going to be a little irritated as well LOL. So a rock may get tossed in their Direction and land at their feet? I say they're lucky it wasn't a brick ha ha. Yes, they can move things. But just as we cannot hurt them, they cannot hurt us either.

I also absolutely and wholeheartedly do not believe in possession. No one can completely take over your space unless you invite a spirit or ghost into your space. Your soul is protected by Heaven at all times and there is no Force in this universe that is greater than God. You are protected at all times. You may feel different in a space and you may feel the energy of a ghost because you are an empath. I feel the personalities of ghosts all the time but it does not mean that they are taking me over by any means. There are definitely times that they feel yucky and so I may feel a little bogged down and simply asked God to place me in a bubble of light so that I'm not feeling the energy in the space or the ghosts in the space around me.

Walking into a room that doesn't feel good does not necessarily mean that there is a ghost in the room. Everything we do in life leaves an imprint of our energy. There's not one place on this Earth that doesn't have some sort of residual energy left behind in that space. Perhaps you just bought a new home and the home just simply has a dreary feel to it? Does that mean that you have a ghost? Not necessarily. You see, the couple that lived there before you may have had a divorce and perhaps there was a lot of fighting and yelling and anger in that space. The imprint of that anger has been left behind in your new home. This is where saging comes in handy. I typically Sage every few months in my home. As I burn the sage and allow the smoke to go from room to room window to Window and Door to Door, I simply say quietly in my mind, "God, please remove all negative thoughts, feelings, emotions and spirits from this space and please replace them with your love and light." I do allow all Heavenly spirits to stay in my home because I simply love them around watching over my family and I to guide and protect us.

Then we have the topic of children seeing ghosts or Spirits. You see, those imaginary friends are not so imaginary for your children who have them. They may be seeing a loved one in spirit and spending time with perhaps your grandmother or a sibling that passed. It's a beautiful thing that I love to embrace when a child sees spirit. I always say that you should write everything down that they are willing to tell you about your loved ones or Spirits they are seeing because they truly are seeing heaven. Children under the age of 7 are very susceptible to seeing heaven and it is very normal. It doesn't mean your child is a psychic, they are just so close to their connection with God and Heaven still that they can simply see spirit. It is not something to fear and of course your children are protected just as you are from heaven. Now, what about a ghost in your home that your child sees? Of course your child may not understand the difference between a spirit and a ghost but you will. Because a ghost tends to come off as angry or grumpy.(I would be angry or grumpy if I missed my ticket to heaven as well and found myself stuck here lol). I still say it's nothing to fear but this is where your opportunity to talk that ghost over to Heaven comes in handy as well. Sit down with your child and Empower your child as well in this case. Your child can absolutely tell the ghost they are not welcome in their space anymore. Your child can tell the ghost that it's not allowed to be in his room at night waking them up. I want you to empower your child because they truly are in control. Teach them to tell the ghost where Heaven is. When my daughter Sydney was 2 years old, she came running out of my bedroom one day and told me that there was an old man in there who told her to "Get Out!". She was crying and trembling and shaking and I was mad. I stomped into my bedroom because I knew the man she was speaking of was a ghost and not truly a real man in life. I slammed the door to my bedroom behind me and I had a not so nice conversation with the ghost in my room. I couldn't see him, but I knew he was there because the fear in my child's eyes was beautiful proof that he was. I said out loud at the top of my lungs, "Don't you ever speak to my child again. This is not your space and you are not to tell my daughter that she does not belong in it. If you want help, then I can tell you how to get to heaven but don't you ever come into my children's space again" Let's just say that he decided he would go to heaven and he never bothered my daughter again. But you see, someone who didn't have my knowledge would have been extremely fearful in that situation for themselves and for their child. I simply put my foot down.

I hope that this answers some of the questions that you may have with activity in and around your home. Remember, Heaven is only three feet off of our floor. Look down where your feet walk and go up three feet from there and that is where our loved ones in heaven walk on Heaven's floor. So, it is very normal to have Spirit around you at all times and it is truly nothing to fear. I think of every ghost that is grounded here as a human just like you and I. They haven't felt the love of Heaven yet because they haven't crossed over. They aren't someone to fear yet lending them a helping hand to Heaven may be all they need. If we all help to support the journey of those around us, this world will certainly be a beautiful place.

6

Let's Talk About Gay, Transgender, And Spirit

I wanted to put a chapter in this book that is near and dear to my heart because I have many Gay and Transgender friends. So much anger and pain in this world comes from this subject and I felt it was necessary to touch upon the subject of being Gay or Transgender in this world. I feel that the more we know about Heaven and Spirit, the less we fear in life. This statement is very true for those who have a fear or anger towards someone who is Gay or Transgender. May I open your mind for a moment to the beauty that lies within them?

I quite often hear a Gay person say that they have felt Gay since Birth. I will then hear Society say that there is "No possible way that they were born Gay"..... I am going to say without a doubt that there is absolutely a way that they have been Gay since birth and the answer to why I can say this without a doubt in my mind is SPIRIT......

You see, we are Eternal in Heaven. We have lived for an Eternity with God before this life and we will live with God for an Eternity again after this life as well. We also live lives in between that Eternity as we choose to. Yes, I believe that we live multiple lives and in multiple roles in those lives. But, we do have a Spirit in Heaven that is unchanged no matter how many lives we live. We are perfect in Heaven and made of God's pure light. Our Spirits also have Genders in Heaven that they keep. Some of us are Beautiful Women Spirits in Heaven. Some of us are Masculine Men in Heaven.

This is the part of the answer where things get so simple that we may not understand why we didn't see it ourselves. Just because we are a Female Spirit in Heaven, does not mean that every life we choose to live is within a Female Body. The same can be said that every Male Spirit in Heaven that lives a physical life may not choose to live every life as a Man. Perhaps there are experiences that a spirit could only learn by living a life in the opposite sex's body.

But, what happens when that Masculine Male Spirit enters a Female body and still remains masculine and attracted to the opposite sex of his spirit (Same sex of his new body), a Woman???? Or, A Female Spirit enters a life as a Male in her Human experience but, as she enters the male body, she still feels all of her feminine qualities that she has had for all eternity, and she (He) is still attracted to men? Should she feel bad for her strong connection to self? They truly are born into bodies that may not feel as though they belong to at times. You can actually see the beautiful spirit within them at times when you see a man with feminine qualities because his spirit is truly female or a female who is so masculine because her spirit within her body is truly a male that even your husband would shy away from an arm wrestling contest with her ha ha....

Does this mean that each and every spirit that lives a life in the body of the opposite sex of their spirit is Gay or Transgender? No, it doesn't. Many of them live a life in the role of the opposite sex without a feeling of attraction to their true spirit in this lifetime that they are living because they have an amazing separation from their memories of themselves in Heaven. But, it doesn't mean those that do feel that pull from the time they were born to love in this world as their spirit loves in Heaven, is wrong.

When a male child likes to dress up in dresses and play in his Mommy's makeup, many people in society will look at that from a place of judgment. When a female woman chooses to live the rest of her physical life as a man because that is where she feels most comfortable, who is she hurting? If a man finds that he is uncomfortable in his own skin and he has an insatiable desire to transform himself completely into a woman, why is he wrong? They are all very connected to their Spirit Self. They are connected to their Souls. They are connected to Heaven.

My point is, they are all beautiful Spirits living a Human experience just as each and every one of us are. There is no right or wrong way of loving in this world as long as we truly love. Each of us is born into the life we chose and on the path we travel for our spirits growth. Please be respectful of those along the way that you meet, for life isn't easy. But, if life were easy, what would we learn from it? They are learning one of the hardest lessons of all through the judgment of others that love in this world simply isn't unconditional. But, what if, just what if everyone began to understand spirit? Life in this world would be filled with unconditional love for everyone and that would surely be a beautiful place to live.

7

Stories Of Healing

*I*n the pages to come, your soul will be filled with the love of Heaven. These are the stories of just a few lives that I have touched with Heaven along my journey. They are the life stories of real people whose loved ones graduated to Heaven before them. These are the stories of reconnecting with those loved ones in Heaven. You will feel love within these words. You may cry tears for these stories may touch your soul. May you find stories in this section that resonate within your life's path so they may bring you healing as they have to these amazing families. May these stories remind you how blessed you are. May these stories give you an insatiable drive to live life to it's fullest potential, for your loved ones are at your side in Heaven cheering you on.

Sit back and relax... You may want a Kleenex or 2 for this chapter. If you are wearing mascara, now may be the time to take it off...

I Met a Little Angel in Heaven tonight... His name is Nolan.....

Nolan was born sleeping into the arms of his Mom and Dad... When Jode reached out to me for a reading, I knew nothing but that she wanted a reading... From the moment that she booked her reading... I had Little Nolan at my side, waiting to talk to his Mommy

Nolan was more than an Angel.. He was an Angel of the Most Special Kind....He also had Down syndrome. When Jode called me, I told her that I had her little boy with me for a week. I told Jode that I would be writing all of her validations down for her, and that she could just focus on crying.. I wasn't sure why I said that, it just came out... And it wasn't long before I knew..

The first thing Nolan told me was #3.. Jode cried as she said, he is my 3rd Child...

Nolan told me that he has 2 sisters with his Mommy, but, he also wanted to acknowledge that he has 4 siblings. Jode confirmed that she has 2 little girls and that Nolan has 2 Step Siblings as well. Nolan told me that one of his Sisters likes to Dress up all the time and that his other sister is opposite of her. Jode laughed and said, that is right. Nolan showed me his sisters playing games together... Jode said, the girls just had the games out the other day... I said, you see,,, You feel as though Nolan misses out on moments with his Sisters and he is letting you know that he doesn't miss out at all...He is with them..

Nolan told me that when he was born, that his Mommy held him on her chest. He said she took his feet in her fingers and almost memorized his little feet with her fingertips... Jode said she held him just as Nolan said and did rub his feet. Nolan then said "She didn't want to let me go"..... Jode cried as she heard these words from her Son..

Nolan showed me a Firefighter and a Fire Truck... Jode told me that Nolan's Daddy is A Firefighter. He also told me in the reading that his Daddy is in Charge of the Fire Station and he showed me his Daddy in the Driver Seat of the Fire Truck as a Symbol of this... Jode, laughed and cried as she said, His Dad is The Captain at the Station... Nolan also told me that his Daddy gave him a Name.. Jode gave me

Goose Bumps, when she told me that his Daddy Nick named him as his "Plug Man"... She said that his Daddy gave him this name to include him in part of his Life as a Firefighter.. You See,, The Plug Man is the Hydrant Guy... The one that takes the Plug... Every Fire Begins and Ends with The "Plug Man".. Nolan knew of this Honorary Name given to him by his Daddy

Nolan told me "My Mommy wears me around her neck. Jode said, he is right; I wear his ashes in my necklace. Nolan told me that his Mommy also wears a wrist band in his Honor... Jode cried as she said, "Yes, I wear two"... Nolan said, She has me next to her in a frame. Jode said, Yes, I am sitting on the bed and his picture is right next to me. Nolan then told me that his Ashes are on the dresser and Jode told me she had Just removed his Necklace with the Ashes in it and set it on the dresser. This was little Nolan's way of letting his Mommy know that he sees her right now.......

When Jode allowed me to share her story, I told her that it would touch so many.. There are so many families out there who have lost babies while giving birth, or miscarriages, Stillborn... Ect... But, the question most asked, is, Did they know I love them? Do they See me? Do they see their Siblings? Nolan's Story will answer that question for so many Moms who have lost their babies as well... Jode wanted to ensure that she was honoring her Son and keeping his Memory alive... I know that he will truly be alive in the Hearts of all who read his Story.... Thank You Nolan..... What a Truly Beautiful Little Soul....

After I shared this story with others, Nolan's Daddy James had a response that is a beautiful way to sum up Daddy's love for Nolan and his beautiful wife Jode:

"PLUG MAN I LOVE YOU BUDDY!!!!. Mommy misses you so much. My heart is so broken for her. Please kiss your Mama each night ok? Till the next alarm sounds"

There is nothing in this world like the love of a Little Girl for her Daddy.... No matter how old she gets, or how their lives change...

Today, Priscilla reached out to me for healing... What she left with was a Heart Filled with love by her Dad In Heaven....

When I connected with her dad, the first thing that he told me to tell her was, "you were enough." He said " I love you very much, I just didn't love myself enough." When I said these words to Priscilla, she broke down in tears. I've then knew why she was crying. He told me that his alcoholism had taken its toll on him, and was the reason he had passed. I knew that he was telling her this because she had questions when he passed.... "Why wasn't I enough as a daughter for you to quit drinking?".... You see.... She Is enough.....

Her Dad talked about Priscilla's Son. He told me that his grandson recently started school. He also told me that his grandson plays baseball and wants his daughter to know that he runs the bases with him. He showed me that he used to give his grandson wheelbarrow rides in life. She confirmed all of this.

He showed me his daughter standing up at his funeral reading a poem at a podium and showed me her son placing flowers at his grave as a way of letting her know that he sees the way that they have honored him since he has passed.

He told me that his little girl needs new tires on her car because the tread is bad. She said he is right. He told me he wants her to be safe and change the tires.

He brought up his Wife and told me she just spent their first Wedding anniversary apart. Priscilla said this was true. He told me that his wife tried to save him and that there was nothing she could have done. He said she wears his wedding ring still. She does..

He said to me... I didn't know how loved I was, until now. I hear that quite often from Spirit who may have led a life that they turned away from those who love them.... you see, he is completely loved... He said, "no matter what kind of Man I was in life, my Little Girl still talks about me as though I am a Hero."... and, he truly always will be a Hero in her eyes...

One of the validations that Priscilla's Dad gave me in her reading was, Priscilla standing up at his funeral and he told me that she read a poem at his funeral... Priscilla shared with me the Beautiful Poem that she read in her Dad's Honor at his Funeral. I would like to share it with all of you, because it truly is Beautiful...

He is gone
You can shed tears that he is gone
Or you can smile because he has lived
You can close your eyes and pray that he will come back
Or you can open your eyes and see all that he has left
Your heart can be empty because you can't see him
Or you can be full of the love that you shared
You can turn your back on tomorrow and live yesterday
Or you can be happy for tomorrow because of yesterday
You can remember him and only that he is gone
Or you can cherish his memory and let it live on
You can cry and close your mind, be empty and turn your back
Or you can do what he would want: smile, open your eyes love and go on

At the end of my day, my Husband and I went out to eat some dinner, because, I had been to busy to eat at dinner time... As we sat there, I looked across the table to my Husband... I knew that I had his Father who is in Heaven hanging out with us and had to have had a funny look on my face as I looked to Jim and said.. I didn't know that your Dad gave you an electric guitar??? I followed that up with, oh; by the way, I have your Dad with me... My Husband said, yeah, my Dad gave me an electric guitar when I was a kid. His Dad went on to bring up more validations that I didn't know.. It is a rule of mine that I will not give validations that I already know.. Evidently, my Father In Law in Heaven Follows my rules too lol.. I learned that my Father in Law was given Medals in the Military... He showed me himself Crouched Down and shooting a 22 rifle with my Husband when my Husband was a child... Jim told me, Yes, My Dad shot My Grandpa's Rifle with me when I was a Kid and gave that Rifle to my Son when he passed away... Jim's Dad then told me that he and My Husband Hunted together as well.. When I told my Husband that his Dad was bringing up their hunting, Jim Laughed and said, Yes, we did hunt... Jim kind of challenged me and said... "Ask my Dad what we hunted"... To which I replied,, He is telling me Pheasant... I could see the Smile in my Husband's eyes as he said, Yes, my Dad and I hunted Pheasant when I was a kid and again when I was an adult...

Then my Husband's Grandpa Stepped forward as well... His Grandpa gave me a reference to Mississippi... Jim said, that could be more than one Grandpa... His grandpa then told me that he was a Farmer, and again, my Husband said, that could still be more than one Grandpa... I said... Well, which one Farmed Cotton? Jim knew then that his Father's Dad was with his Dad in Heaven, as we were talking...

Jim's Grandpa on his Mom's side of the family wanted to chime in as well...He also gave me a Farming reference... but, not just garden-ing.. He made me feel like he harvested Crops in his Farming... He had a Group of Hunting Dogs with him that were Howling up a storm and Jim said, Oh Yes, that is my Grandpa.. He always had Hunting dogs... His Grandpa showed me that he had written letters to my Husband in life... My Husband said, yes, my Grandpa wrote me letters when I was Stationed away in The Air Force.

People ask me all the time if I get messages for myself from my family... The answer is No... Why? Because I don't need them.. I know my family is safe in Heaven's arms. I don't need Faith Restored, or Healing.. But, I can tell you, that it feels pretty amazing to give the Man I love, Messages from his Loved Ones from time to time, when they decide to interrupt dinner lol... What a Cool way to end the Day!

Debra asked if her Son Michael could sit in for the reading, and I wasn't about to Let Nicole's Little Brother miss out on this Christmas Gift from his Sister in Heaven....

Nicole came through with validations of her passing for her Mom. She told me that she had a Head Injury that impacted her passing. Debra told me that yes, her daughter, Nicole, had been injured in Iraq and she had health issues with this injury that led to her passing after she came home...

Nicole wanted her Mom and Brother to know that she has the little Dog with her in Heaven. She said she also has the Collie Dog that passed as well that belonged to her Grandparents. She then showed me that her Grandpa was with her in Heaven. She told me that her Grandpa was in the Military and he showed me himself with a Cigarette. Debra knew that this was her Dad at Nicole's side. She was Happy to hear they were together. They had lost a small family dog that was important to Nicole when she was younger as well and the Collie was her parent's Dog.

Nicole gave me a Makeup reference and Deb said.... Nicole was a Makeup artist in life. Deb said that Nicole had taught her how to put on Eyelashes and makeup as well.

Nicole told me that her little Brother Michael was going to be getting his driver's license soon. Michael said yes... She wanted him to know that she will still be with her little brother as he does his road test. She said she wouldn't miss it for the world. Michael was taken back when she said this; because, his sister had told him that she would take him out to teach him drive before his test.

Nicole then showed me that her Mom was recently looking at her Photo Album. Nicole said that when her Mom was looking at the albums, that she found a Hand Written Letter that she had written to Mom... Deb cried, as she said YES.... Deb said that she had never seen this note before and she recently found it as she looked through Nicole's albums. She included a picture of the note her daughter wrote her and I can tell you, it will take your breath away......

Nicole told me that she had been honored in the Military. Deb said that her daughter had been honored. She said that her daughter's name

was put on a wall where they life. She had also been honored by The
Patriot Guard after she passed with a Plaque.

Nicole told me that there are memorial tattoos in her honor. She
wanted to send her love to the people who had these tattoos. Deb told
me that Nicole's sisters have matching memorial tattoos in her honor..
Nicole then told me that her Brother is planning to get one as well and
Michael said he plans to get the tattoo is sisters have for Nicole. Nicole
then told me that her Mom will be getting me a memorial tattoo for her
as well, but, that it will be different from the others. Deb said, that she
does plan to get a tattoo and it will be different from the others.

Nicole told me that her Mom lights candles for her. Deb said that she
does keep a candle burning for her daughter every day. Nicole wanted to
thank her Mom for lighting the candles.

Nicole told me that her Mom and Brother just decorated her Grave
with a Christmas Tree and other decorations and I could hear 16 year
old Michael say ... WOW.... We did.... Michael said that you could see his
sister's decorations above anyone else's decorations where she is buried.

Nicole said that the family played games together today..... They did
play games at their Christmas gathering... This was Nicole's way of letting her family know that she was there to play games with them.

Nicole told me that her Mom is reading a book for her... Deb said, I
am reading "Waking Up in Heaven"...... I would say that Nicole is Right ♥

There were many more validations that came through during our
reading... She loves her Family and will watch over and guide them from
Heaven..... Her Little Brother will always has an Angel that he can carry
with him in life, no matter where the road takes him.... Deb will always
have her beautiful Little girl nearby, comforting her Mom and loving
her from Heaven with her Pa at her side....

FARA GIBSON

When Phyllis and Blair (Husband and Wife) called me for their reading last night.... I knew it would be Blessed.... I had asked God for a sign on my way home from work yesterday, to let me know that I would bring them healing and a Huge Crane (Bird) flew over my truck in that moment... I don't know how many of you are familiar with Arizona lol.. But, Crane's are not a common sight here ha ha... This was going to be a Blessed Evening. As I told Phyllis and Blair of the Crane... They said that their last name, translated in a different language, actually means... Bird ♥

As I began my reading with Phyllis and Blair, their Beautiful Daughter in Heaven McKenna, stepped forward.... She snapped my fingers, as I asked her how she passed... She told me she was here one moment and gone the next. She said that she had passed in a Car Accident.... In that moment.. Phyllis and Blair, knew that their Daughter was with us...

One of the first things that McKenna showed me was a Drawn Portrait of herself... She made me feel like Mom (Phyllis) had this portrait... When I asked about this, Phyllis told me that she does in fact have a Portrait of her Beautiful Daughter in a Memorial Tattoo that she recently had done. This was McKenna's way of letting Mom know that she still sees her and Thanks her for Honoring her with the tattoo... McKenna told me that there is another Memorial Tattoo done for her as well and her parents told me that her Brother has a memorial tattoo as well.. This was McKenna's way of sending love to her Brother.

McKenna wanted her parents to know that she has a little dog and a bigger dog with her in Heaven. Phyllis and Blair said that those are family dogs and they were happy to hear they are with McKenna.

McKenna told me that someone just did a balloon release for her and her parents said they had just released lanterns for her very recently... (I don't have a symbol for Lanterns in my rolodex, which is why she showed me balloons... Kenna and I just added a new symbol to my rolodex for lanterns, Thanks Kenna)

54

McKenna showed me that her Mom was hanging something for her for Christmas and Phyllis gasped as she said that she had just bought an Angel Ornament to hang for McKenna.

Blair asked if anyone was with McKenna as we did the reading and as I asked who was with her, Blair's Father stepped forward from Heaven. He told me that he smoked in life… He gave me a Military reference with himself and I could hear the Hunting Dogs Howling with his Dad in Heaven… Blair knew this to be his Dad with the Hunting Dogs and his Dad did smoke in life and was in the Military. With the Hunting reference, Blair's dad told me that he hunted Birds as well.. Blair reminisced in that moment and told me what a Good Shot his Dad was in life… It was a Beautiful Moment between Father and Son…

McKenna Then Interrupted her Grandpa talking to her Dad to tell me that she would Shoot Guns in life with her Dad and she Referred to Blair as a Hunter as well… Blair was choked up to hear this from his Little Girl… She went on to tell me that she and Blair had gone shooting together shortly before she passed…. Blair said he and his Daughter had gone shooting and he Chuckled as he told me that she may have been a better Shot than her Brothers lol……

McKenna told me that she did some Modeling in life and with this, she showed me an Image of herself with her face upturned to the sky with her arms in the air…. As I asked her parents about this, they told me that they used that exact image of her for their memorial!!! They were kind enough to include it in the pictures that they sent me for this story, to share it with all of you… It is STUNNING!!!! Her Parents said they even love the silly pictures that show her beautiful personality and I have to agree…. I love them too!!!

McKenna told me that her Parents are Lobbying in her Honor and they are… They are trying to ensure that no one else looses their life in that intersection where there is a Stop sign on one side and a yellow caution on the other.. McKenna had been T-Boned in that intersection…….

McKenna also told me that there was something being named after her in her Honor and her parents told me that there is a Food Bank being run in her Honor, because it was Important to McKenna that no one went Hungry in life.... What a Beautiful Soul

The last thing McKenna showed me was for her Fiancé.... Who she previously in the reading wanted to send her love to.... She showed me a Blanket or quilt made of her clothing and made me feel like this was something Mom was doing... Phyllis told me that she was planning to have a Quilt Made for her Fiancé, so that he could have something of McKenna's to wrap up in. What a Beautiful Gesture from Phyllis for her Daughter's Love..

Phyllis has been on my page for some time... This Reading is Close to my Heart, as I have seen the Progress of Phyllis's Healing and Growth in the short time that she has been here... Readings always happen in Perfect Heaven's Timing for the Healing of the Loved Ones here and McKenna did a Beautiful Job Healing her Mom and Dad's hearts last night. I don't think they doubted before that McKenna was watching over them... But, when you are doing a reading for someone and the Lights in the room they are sitting in begin to Flicker numerous times.... You have to Smile and say... Thanks McKenna

Phyllis and her husband Blair have previously had a phone reading with me. In that previous reading, their beautiful daughter McKenna who passed instantly in a vehicle accident came through for her parents. This time, Phyllis and Blair would be flying into Arizona and wanted to book an in-person reading with me while they were here from out of state. It is a reading that will forever be in my Heart.

McKenna had told me in a previous reading that her parents started a foundation in her honor and they had. You see, McKenna felt that no one should ever go hungry and she felt as long as they had peanut butter, that they would be well. Phyllis and Blair began a foundation in McKenna's honor called McKenna's Open Cupboard after her passing to take up collections for peanut butter for those who were hungry or in need so that no one would go hungry in McKenna's reach. When I began the reading last night, McKenna told me that her parents began to collect a second item for her foundation besides just the peanut butter. Phyllis and Blair said they had begun to collect jelly now as well. McKenna told me that her parents were doing drives in numerous places for the peanut butter. She said that her friends have been helping with donations as well and she wanted to send for love to them for their help. McKenna was then showing me that her picture is outside and she said that it is a permanent fixture. She made me feel as though her picture is affixed to metal. She also showed me that there is a white sign with her name on it. She said, please tell my parents how proud I am of them for all they have done for me. Phyllis showed me that McKenna's picture is in fact affixed to the outside of a large metal storage container and to the right of her beautiful picture is her name on a white sign. This storage container houses the peanut butter collected for McKenna's Foundation. It was beautiful to know that she isn't missing it from heaven.

McKenna told me that her family attended a Candle Light Vigil in honor of her recently. Phyllis said that she and Blair had attended a Candle Light Vigil for McKenna just last month in December. McKenna said there was music at the Vigil and she wanted her parents to know how Thankful she was that they did this in her honor and she was at their side.

McKenna told me that her dad has a tattoo in honor of her now and she said my name is on Dad's tattoo. As I asked Blair about this, he showed me a tattoo he had recently received for his daughter and on this tattoo was the name that he called her in life, "My Boo Bug." McKenna told me that her mom had recently gotten more tattoos in honor of her as well and she made me feel as though Mom has a tattoo for her on her wrist now also. Phyllis stood up and took her jacket off that was covering this beautiful tattoo that she has on her wrist now in honor of both McKenna and McKenna's fiancé who passed shortly after McKenna did.

McKenna wanted me to tell her parents that she has a new dog in heaven with her recently. She showed me this dog with a really cool bandana on himself and made me feel as though he was old and sick and lumpy in life. Phyllis and Blair were both relieved to find out that their precious male dog who was old and sick and lumpy was with McKenna.

They said that this dog not only loved to wear bandanas in life, but that he and another dog would play a back and forth game with a scarf that they loved as well. They sent a picture of their precious family member and in the picture, he is sporting one of his favorite bandanas.

Blair wanted to know if he could ask his little girl a question I told him he was absolutely free to ask a question and of course it would be up to McKenna to be able to answer it for me through my abilities. Blair understood this and he simply wanted to know if his daughter was in Canada with him on his trip fairly recently? I told Blair that as he asked this question, McKenna was taking me out on a fishing boat. Blair's eyes got Wide as I said this and he said please go on. McKenna said that her dad had caught a huge fish but she showed me herself down in the water hooking a fish onto her Dad's hook for him from heaven. Again Blair wanted to ask a question and he said, can she tell you anything about the fish? I told Blair that as he asked this question, McKenna was showing me the color red. Blair threw his hands up over his eyes to catch the tears that were falling. I said, was there a red fish? Blair said yes, there was a red snapper fish. I said, she is also showing you very large fish as well? Blair said, I hooked a red snapper fish without even knowing it and it then became bait for a much larger lingcod fish. Blair said that when he pulled the fish from the water, the lingcod had a red snapper fish hanging out of its mouth! He had caught 2 Fish At The Same Time!!! Blair fought the tears that were falling from his eyes as he realized in that moment that without a doubt, his little girl had been on his fishing trip with him in Canada. He sent me a picture of the fish inside of the fish and I have to say it was an ugly fish that became one of the coolest validations I have ever given from Heaven!

McKenna then took me into her bedroom and made me feel as though her mom has been spending some time in there. She told me that Mom is trying to make her room more beautiful and she wants her to know that she's with her in this difficult time. Phyllis told me that she has been folding things and straightening up in McKenna's room recently. McKenna then took a headband off of her head and wanted me to hand it to her mom. Phyllis said, I took all of her head bands after she passed in the accident.

McKenna wanted me to tell her parents how very much she loves them. She wanted them to know how very proud she is of all they have done for her since her passing. McKenna also wanted to send her love to her brothers as well and Phyllis and Blair said they would be sure to send her love to them. McKenna also had numerous family members with her in heaven who also came through during this reading but, we will post that story in a separate story so that McKenna can shine in this Story with Love for her family. Phyllis and Blair and I each hugged one another when this reading was through. As Blair grabbed a hold of my shoulders, he said to me, I don't know how we would have gotten through this without you. Phyllis wanted to give me a gift before I left that reading. She had purchased me a Map of the World. As she handed it to me, she said, "You get to reach people all over the World and I thought you might like this Map to see all the the places these people are from. I couldn't help but cry as she handed it to me. She had no idea the impact this Map would have on my Heart and Soul when she purchased it. You see, I had an opportunity to ask a Question of Psychic/Medium John Edwards when My Husband Surprised me with front row seats to one of his events a few year back. As I asked John, "Is there One reading that stands out to you from all of the rest? One reading that you remember the most of all of the readings you have done?" I could see John look inward to his Soul as I asked this question. John Edwards answered me by saying "Wow, No one has ever asked me anything like that before. I don't know that any reading stands out above the rest because each Reading has become like a Road Map all over the World for the People that I have touched along my path with Healing"..... Those words have forever stayed in my Heart and I too have begun my very own road map of Healing. This Map that Phyllis handed me was a Sign for me with an impact that she may never understand. I look forward to filling this Map with Love and Healing until the day that I take my final breath on this path. I had tears running down most of my drive home with a smile upon my face and in my soul. All I could think to say was, "Way to go and McKenna."

I did a reading today for Vicki and her daughter Megan. As they reached out to me for their reading, I felt as though I had a young man with a Head Related passing with me in Spirit waiting to send his love to them.

Tyler (In Heaven) first brought up the Hair.... I asked the girls if they had just had their hair done, and they both told me no. I was a bit confused at this, as Tyler kept telling me about the hair.... Little did I know, that Vicki and Megan had Brought Tyler's Hair with them to hold during our reading....

Tyler told me that he had passed in a Car Accident. He made me feel as though a Hispanic Man hit him. He told me that the Man that hit him was not driving legally and that is why he left the scene of the accident.... The women validated to me after telling them this, that, Tyler was killed in a Hit and Run accident... The Man that hit him was a Hispanic male who was driving illegally....

Tyler showed me that he has an Infant Girl in his arms and made me feel as though she belonged to Megan... Megan cried as she realized her Brother has her Baby that she miscarried, safe in his arms.

Tyler also showed me that there is an infant boy coming in the family. He told me that this Boy will share a name with him.. The women told me that Tyler has another sister who is Pregnant with a baby boy and she is planning on naming him after Tyler.... What a Beautiful Gesture by his Sister and Tyler thought so too.

Tyler acknowledged that there is a Man who carries him on his chest.. Megan Gasped as she realized that Tyler was speaking of her Husband who recently got a Memorial Tattoo for Tyler on His Chest..

Tyler told me that he was recognized at school for something and the ladies told me that the school had done a fundraiser in his honor. He also told me that there had been a car wash in his honor as well and there had been..

Tyler told me to tell his Mom and Sister that He Met Jesus at the Scene of the Accident.. He wanted them to know that he was no longer in his Body as he was taken to the hospital... He watched from outside of his Body as they took him to the Hospital... He said that His Beautiful Girlfriend had Climbed into bed with him as he laid there in the Hospital bed as he was passing... Megan and Vicki told me that his Girlfriend had climbed into bed with him in the hospital, They had hoped he hadn't suffered. He truly didn't.. He watched from a place of pure love.. He said.. "It wouldn't have been any fun to stay in that silly body during that"... So, he didn't...

    I could go on and on with this reading and the love he sent to so many people... But, the True Message is LOVE.... Tyler is in Heaven... He is Happy and pain free... He watches over his Loved Ones and I can tell you that his Sense of humor is still intact, because, he brought up a Pot Smoking Reference and got a good giggle out of making me feel a bit loopy for a moment... He even referenced his Best Friend who has his Pipe lol... Got to Love a Spirit with an Amazing SPIRIT ♥

I asked God as my feet hit the floor this morning, to "Please help me to Heal Someone today...." I love that God answers those prayers for me....

When Jennifer called me for her reading, I could hear the stress in her voice... It wasn't long after her reading started, that I understood why..... Jennifer's Son in Heaven came through.... His Passing, was a Suicide..... The Love this young Spirit sent to his Mom was overwhelming....

Her Son told me that he was in the Military.. His mom sobbed as she said that he was.... He told me that he earned Medals in the Military and that his Mom has these medals now. She said, that her son had never told her about the medals in life because he was so Humble and it wasn't until he passed, that she learned what a Hero he was. He showed me his Military Boots and made me feel as though Mom has a Pair and then he showed me a pair of boots on display... His Mom said that she had 2 pairs of his Boots and she kept one pair for herself and the other pair was given to his Sergeant, and his Sergeant set them up on Display.

Her Son told me that his Mom has his picture with her right now. She cried as she said she does. He told me that his Mom Just visited his Grave and placed a Plant on it. Jennifer said she visited her Son Just before our reading and she just put a Christmas Tree on his Grave yesterday.

Her Son told me that his Funeral was big. He said he had been buried in full Military Uniform. Jennifer confirmed that he was. He told me that his Mom and others had placed items in his casket at the funeral and she said they had. He told me that there was a Big Picture of him in his Military Uniform on display at the funeral and then showed me that it was going up in the house... He joked that his Step Dad still has to hang it up......Jennifer told me that they are going to hang it above the fireplace and that it is waiting there for her Husband to hang...

He told me that his Mom has a Metal Engraving from him. She said she does have an engraved Necklace from her Son that he had given her in life. He also told me that his mom has a Bracelet and Ring of his as well.. She said that she does have his bracelet and she has his High School Ring...

He told me that he has younger brothers and wanted to send his love to them. He even showed me that the little one dressed up in military camo.. Jennifer said that she had just bought camo pants for her youngest son with his big brother in mind..

I asked her Son to please tell me about his passing... All I could say to Jennifer repeatedly was I'm sorry..... Her Son showed me that he had Shot himself... When I asked for his reasoning, he said.... It wasn't planned... I didn't think it through.. He took responsibility. He showed me his Friend that found him and frantically tried to help him..... He said there was nothing he could have done to save me... I couldn't have been loved any more than I was.... No one should feel guilty or as though they could have done something different to save me.... Jennifer said that His Best friend had gone into the bathroom, and when he came out, her son was already gone.... They didn't have a reason why....

I know that her Son couldn't give me a reason in his reading, because, he was so completely Loved... He had everything going for him... Our Men and Women in the military put their Life on the line for us each and every day... The things that they go through in the Military can change their perception when they come home..... This young Man in my eyes, Graduated from This World as A HERO......... For, although he did not give his life in battle overseas.... He gave his life in Battle here at home ♥

From the moment that Tina contacted me to schedule a reading, I felt as though, I would be connecting her with a child in Heaven... I was right......

Her Son Tyty immediately told me that he was 1 of 3 children. He said there are 2 boys and 1 girl. Tina sobbed as she said yes...

Tyty told me that his Mom tried to do all that she could to save his life. He said there was nothing she could have done. He kept telling me that it was unexpected for him to pass. There were no signs prior to his passing. He was right! No Mother expects her young child to pass from a heart attack.....

Tyty told me that his Mom has a bracelet that she wears in his honor. Tina confirmed that memorial bracelets had been made in his honor. Tyty told me that his Mom has a memorial tattoo with his name on her. She said, yes, I have 2 memorial tattoos, one with his name and one with his nickname.

Tyty told me that his funeral was huge! He said the whole school came! He said, "They did all of this for me!" He showed me people at the funeral placing items in his casket. Tina said that numerous people placed items with him. Tyty then told me that his Mom placed a Necklace with him and he Thanked her for that. Tina said she placed a Crucifix necklace on her son. Tyty told me that his Mom did something with his hair for him after he passed as well. Tina said, I hope he isn't mad at me, because I cut some of his hair to save it. I assured her that her Son isn't Mad. It was just his way of letting her know that he sees her even after he has passed.

I asked Tina about a picture of Tyty with a candle on the side of it, with other memorial items around it.... I don't even know if she realized, until she reads this story, that the picture she sent me to share with all of you after the reading was over, is the exact picture he was showing me smile emoticon

Tyty told me that he was just about to start driving, but, never had a chance to get his license. Tina said, yes. Tyty was just 16 when he passed away ... He had begun to learn to drive and was going to get his license soon.

He told me that his Mom talks to him in her prayers every night. He wants her to know he hears her each night... He will always hear her.. He will always watch over her. In the moments that she feels she can't go on without him, she needs to know that he is there, protecting her.....

Thank You Tina for sharing your Son with us today. He has such a beautiful Soul. His story will Heal so many Moms Hearts today.

Wanda and her family booked a Skype reading with me in advance. I had Previously done a reading for Wanda and her family, so this would be their second reading. In a previous reading, Wanda's Son Larry in Heaven came through. Her son had passed suddenly and unexpectedly. A few hours before the reading, I felt her son Larry join me in spirit for a moment and he said, "My Brother Is Here!" I didn't understand what this meant, but, I felt compelled to message this validation to Wanda prior to getting on the Skype Screen together. (You see, I knew that Wanda and her family would be joining me for the reading, but, I didn't know WHO in her family would be joining us. I wanted to message her before I could See on screen who was there since her Son was telling me the validation in advance) Wanda said to me, His Brother in Law wasn't there last time, but will be tonight. I thought it was pretty cool that Larry was acknowledging his brother would be joining us before I could see him on the screen when we started!

Larry told me that he had joined someone in the family to go hunting. Wanda and her daughter on the screen laughed and looked over to Larry's Brother in law who was off screen and said, Yes, he just went hunting today.

I said, Well, Larry says he didn't get anything out on the hunt ha ha. The family giggled a little and I could hear Larry's Brother off-screen say that Larry was correct and he didn't get anything on his hunt. I loved that Larry referenced a validation for his brother to let him know that he was with him from Heaven. Larry also suddenly made me feel like I was wearing Camouflage as well and Wanda said, Yes, his Brother is wearing Camo.

Larry then made me look at his sister on the screen and say, "Why does he tell me to say to you, I've Got Dibbs on The Pie". His sister fought back tears as she said, I am making his favorite pie. I said, Your Brother says you set an extra place for him at the table for the holiday. His sister said, I was just counting place settings needed today for our Thanksgiving Dinner and I was planning to set a place for him at the table as I did at a previous Holiday dinner after his passing. I told his sister that her Brother Loves and Appreciates how she is honoring him in setting the place for him. Larry also said there would be another young girl who wasn't here at the reading but would be joining the family for Thanksgiving that he wanted to send his love to as well. Wanda said, Yes, his cousin is coming and we will send his love to her.

There was a young girl sitting on Wanda's lap as we did the reading and I looked at her on the screen and said to Wanda, Larry says that is his Niece.

Wanda said, She sure is. I said, He tells me that his niece was just playing checkers? Wanda shook her head because she wasn't aware of any checkers play and Wanda's daughter looked a bit confused as well. I then heard Larry's Brother in law off screen say that he had his daughter at a coffee shop That Morning and his daughter was playing with a Checkers Game at the coffee shop!!! No One Knew This!!!! But, Larry Did! Larry then showed me his Niece shooting at a target and made me feel she was doing "Target Practice". Wanda said, she has been shooting her bow and arrow at targets for practice. I loved that this little girl's Uncle in Heaven was making it clear that he watches over his niece from Heaven.

Larry showed me 2 hamsters in his hands in Heaven. Wanda and her daughter began to laugh because they had 2 hamsters when they were younger and the hamsters are now in Heaven. (Yes, we even reunite with our little pets in Heaven)

Larry showed me his Dad working on a Pickup Truck with tools to fix a truck and Dad said, Yes, he had just worked on a truck for a family member that was having trouble. Larry made me laugh as he told me to say, "I thought a Dipstick was something you called someone in life" Dad laughed and said Oh Yes, That is Larry!!! He didn't work on vehicles at all and never even changed his own oil in his vehicle hahahahahaha Larry showed me that he has a large Black Lab type dog with him in Heaven that belongs to a friend of his in life. He wanted to send his love to this friend as well as tell his friend that he had his Dog safe with him in Heaven who passed.

I then got a validation that I argued with Larry about for a bit before I said it to his family, but, hey, who am I to argue with spirit and Larry was adamant about this validation. I said to Wanda, Larry is showing me little Frogs or Toads and he makes me feel like he sent you a little Frog/toad as a sign recently? Wanda's jaw dropped as I said this and I could hear Dad laughing off screen. Wanda's daughter had no clue what Mom and Dad were so stunned about, but, it wasn't long before we were all laughing with our jaws open! Wanda said that recently, she and her husband had found a Small Toad/Frog in the TOILET in their bathroom in their home!!!!!!!! Okay, Where the heck else does a Frog in the toilet of your home come from besides Heaven hahahahahahahaha!!! I laughed and said, Well, that sure isn't a validation that you could make up hahahahahahahaha!!!

Larry then slipped something like a watch on my wrist and took me to Mom, and I asked Wanda if she had something on her wrist for Larry? Wanda began to cry as she pulled her sleeve back on her shirt to reveal a watch of Larry's that she had hidden before our reading began and she had asked her Son to please bring it up. I then said, He tells me that someone has one of his hats out as well. As I said this, Larry's sister started moving a blanket or jacket off of her lap and she pulled out Larry's Hat and put It on her head. She said, I didn't tell anyone that I put his hat on my lap under this before we started! She too had asked Larry to acknowledge the hat she had hidden and he did!!!!! I then said, He also says someone carries him in their Jeans Pocket? Wanda reached into her pocket and pulled out a bag that held her son's ashes inside of it. She said she takes him everywhere she goes and she had him in her pocket the whole reading!

I said to Wanda, Is there a reason that your son is handing me a bouquet of balloons for you? Wanda began to cry as she said that she had booked this reading for her Birthday because she wanted more than anything in this world to speak to her Son again on her Birthday! I said to Wanda, Happy Birthday From Heaven.......................

This reading was filled with amazing examples of spirit that will inspire love in so many. I was blessed to be a part of this family for an evening to share the love between each of them.

Karren and her husband Dan called me for a reading today via Skype that Karren booked months ago. I previously did a phone reading for Karren, but, this time we would be able to see one another as we did her second reading and her husband Dan would be present for the first time in a reading.

Karren's son Drew had come through in the reading I previously did for Karren. It is always so amazing to get to meet these amazingly beautiful spirits again and ask for all new validations that they didn't give me in the last reading.

As we began the reading, Drew immediately took me back to his passing. I already knew how Drew passed because he had previously told me that he had taken his own life by Suicide with a Gun. But, Drew was giving me more than he had given me before. Drew showed me that he had an argument with his girlfriend the day of his passing. Karren and Dan said this was true. I said, Drew is showing me that she was trying to "Repo" a car from him? He is making me feel like she was taking a car back? Karren and Dan cried as they recalled their Son taking his girlfriend's car back because of an argument they had and Drew's truck was not running at the time. Drew told me that he took his life in the home of his girlfriend. He said that he took his life in her home in hopes that she would find him because he was upset. He made me feel as though his girlfriend had her daughter with her when she found him and he never intended for this little girl to see him this way. He went on to have me tell his parents, "Your son did not give you any indications that he was going to take his life that day when he left your home. He wants you to stop looking for signs that weren't there that he would take his life that day. He didn't plan this in advance and he truly did it on a whim as he was going through a difficult time." Karren and Dan broke down in tears together as I said these words and they both said they felt so responsible for not being able to stop him from taking his life.

Drew told me that his Dad was recently in the hospital for trouble with his health in his chest/heart area. Drew showed me that Dad and Mom had to travel for this visit to the hospital. He said Mom had to travel back and forth to see Dad because of work. He wanted his parents to know that he closely watched over Mom and Dad during this time from Heaven. Dan cried because he felt his son at his side during his hospital stay and it was amazing to know that his feelings were real. Karren did have to travel back and forth for work while Dan was in the hospital some distance from their home. Drew said that he was Thankful for Dan in his life. He wanted to Thank Dan for stepping into the shoes of being his Father in life even though he was not his biological father. Dan's tears ran down his cheeks as he told me that he was proud to be Dan's Father in life.

Drew said that his Mom is writing letters to him and he wanted her to know he is getting her letters in Heaven. Karren said that she writes a blog for her Son and writes to him almost daily.

Drew then told me that the shirt his Mom was wearing right now is his. Karren laughed as she said, Yes, this is my Son's shirt. Drew made me feel like he handed me one of his ball caps to put on my head and as I explained this to Karren, she reached out of reach of the Skype Camera and she picked up a ball cap of her son's and placed it on her head. Karren said, "I asked him to bring this hat up before we started and I placed this hat at my feet out of view! Way to go Drew!!! Drew also showed me that his Mom had just worn his Basketball shorts. Karren said, yes, I did just wear his basketball shorts! Drew showed me a balloon release for his Angelversary. Karren said, We just had his Angelversary less than 2 weeks ago and we did a balloon release and I wore his Basketball shorts to the release. I said, Drew says some of his friends were there also and Karren said, yes they were. Drew also showed me his friends lighting candles in his honor. Karren said, yes, they did a candle light vigil for him after he passed.

Drew showed me a ring of his own and made me feel as though his ExGirlfriend was giving his family trouble in recovering items of his, but he told me that he made sure that his Mom and Dad got this ring back all on his own from Heaven. Karren and Dan laughed and cried at this validation because when Karren looked through all of her son's things, the ring was not there. She said she searched everywhere. Karren went on to say that she found the ring in the ash tray of her son's truck, but she knew without a doubt that she had looked in his ash tray and that ring wasn't there before! She wanted to believe that her Son had made it appear from Heaven and this was beautiful proof of that without even having to ask the question!!! Drew went on to tell me that his Mom is driving that truck of his now since he passed. Karren said, yes, I am. Drew showed me that his things are still hanging from the rear view mirror in the truck. Karren said, yes, there is no way I could take them down. Karren then said, I still have his receipts in the truck that he left! Well, Since Karren told me that she has the receipts, that was no longer anything I could tell her from Drew, so, I asked Drew if he could tell me about one of the receipts that his Mom mentioned. I said, "Karren, is one of those receipts from Taco Bell?" Karen and Dan began to laugh hysterically as Karren said, YES!!!!! Ha Ha Good Save Drew!!!!

Drew told me that his Mom is framing pictures and paintings in honor of him, lots of them. He showed me that if I look around his Mom's living room (I couldn't see the room on the skype screen), that there are Staggered pictures at all levels on the walls of him at all ages that surround the walls in the room. Karren said, Oh Yes, there are pictures of him all over the walls at all levels and they go all the way around the room! She also said she is making a bunch of special pictures of Drew and framing them as well and they are personalized.

Drew said that his Mom has potted plants in honor of him still. He then showed me what in my mind's eye looked like flowers or something colorful growing up out of the potted plants? Karren said she does have plants given in Drew's honor after his passing and she had gone to the store and bought the Solar Powered lights to place in the pots that are colorful. When she sent me a picture of the pots after the reading with the lights in them, I had to laugh because it was exactly why I was confused as to why It looked like there were flowers growing up out of the potted plants. I just knew it was beautiful and it was!!!

I received a note with the pictures that Karren sent me that put tears upon my cheeks. It said, " Thank you for the most amazing reading. You gave much healing to both Dan and I today. We have been struggling with his death and now we know the truth. We are both going to put the guilt behind us." Wow, I can't even put into words how it feels to hear that from parents who's children are in Heaven..... I am humbled by their Growth.

Last week, an amazing Man on my page gifted a reading anonymously on my page and Sharon was drawn to receive that gift. Yesterday, Sharon joined me on the phone for her reading. When I said, "How are you today?", Sharon said, "I'm Nervous". I laughed just a little and said, "Oh Sharon, I will take Nervous and just wait to see how we turn that Into Love." Sharon told me that a friend and niece would be sitting at her side while we did the reading and I explained to her that it would be fine to have them sit it. But, I always let clients know that if they choose to have someone sit with them, that it is out of my control if someone comes through for them from Heaven as well, so to please ensure that each person wants to hear from the same loved ones in Heaven as you. Sharon understood and so we began.

I told Sharon that I had a Male to her side coming through who made me feel like a Husband for her. He told me that he was sick at the end of his life and gave me a cancer reference in my lung area. Sharon said, yes, my Husband Jerry passed from Lung Cancer. Jerry said that his wife took care of him through his illness and he wanted to Thank Her for all she had done for him. He showed me that Sharon and 3 others were at his side when he passed to Heaven and he gave me a reference that was very clear. Jerry made me feel as though he had swallowing issues at the end of his life because he was Intubated. He said that his wife had very difficult decisions to make at the end of his life and he wanted her to know that she did everything just right. He said she honored his wishes and he knows how hard that was for her. He wanted to Thank her for being so strong. Sharon understood this message well and said out loud through her tears, "Thank You Jerry" He showed me his beautiful wife touching his chest and he said, "She felt my last Heart Beat" and I want her to know that I saw this in Spirit at her side. Sharon cried as she said that she had felt her husband's last heart beat when he passed to Heaven.

Jerry told me that he has daughters that he wanted to send his love to and he showed me 2 daughters for Sharon. Jerry then told me "I was outnumbered by all of the girls". Sharon began to laugh because her husband was right and she said, Jerry would always say, "I am outnumbered by the girls in this family". She was sensing her Husband's personality coming through in the reading and so was I. I said, Oh, he's gonna be fun ha ha. Jerry showed me his Grandkids dressed in his Tshirts with Shirts hanging down to their legs because they were too big on them. Sharon said, yes, our Grandkids all wore his shirts after he passed in honor of him and I have a picture of it! He told me that his wife is wearing his shirts as well and she said that she is.

Jerry then made me giggle a little when I used his words to say, "Shit!, She moved all the furniture around. She Moved the Couch too!" hahahaha.... Sharon laughed and laughed as she said, Yes she had moved all of the furniture around and she went on to say that she moved the furniture around so much when Jerry was living that he would always say, "You never know where the couch is going to be with her!" Hahahahaha.... Jerry then said, She got rid of my old ugly recliner too. Sharon laughed some more and said, oh yes, I got rid of that chair. I stopped Sharon for just a moment and said, "You See, Your Nervous is gone and you are feeling your Husband, and That is why I do this".

Jerry then told me that he had a large "Hank " earring in his left ear for some time during a midlife crisis hahahaha.... I was beginning to really like this guy hahaha. Sharon laughed some more with her tears and said oh yes, he did and it was during a midlife crisis hahaha. Jerry told me that his wife had saved many love notes he had written to her in life. Sharon said, yes, I have our love notes saved that he gave me. I then blushed a little before I had to spit out Jerry's next validation haha.... I said, "Jerry tells me that some of those notes were a little DIRTY" hahahahaha.... Sharon and I both got a good laugh out of that one when she agreed that in their earlier days, he had written a few fun notes that she has saved. Believe me, I tried to get her to send a copy for a validation with this story, but...... Ha Ha, No I didn't, those are their notes he he he... I just thought it was a fun validation hahahaha.

Jerry then told me that his wife wears him on her skin in a tattoo and he showed me that his name was at the bottom of the tattoo. Sharon said, yes, I have a tattoo on my back that says, "When a loved one becomes a memory, The memory becomes a Treasure, JERRY."

Jerry then told me that he has a Tan colored, Midsized dog with him in Heaven as well. Sharon said, "Oh Wow", Yes!!!! Sharon's precious Girl was at her Husband's side in Heaven. I then said, "Omg, What was that!?" Sharon got a little quiet for me to explain what I had just seen hahaha.... I said, I just saw a Rodent run by in my vision and I then saw cats chasing the mouse in Heaven. Sharon said again, Oh Wow!! Sharon said that she had asked her husband to bring up the Mouse reference because she was so afraid of mice and they had an issue with mice at one time and their cats who are now in Heaven would chase and catch the mice in the house hahaha... I said, Well, they must have caught a few because I see a few cats chasing mice in Heaven right now hahaha....

Jerry said I should say "Hello Neighbor!" As I said this, Sharon said that the friend who joined her for this reading is their neighbor ha ha. Jerry showed me that he enjoyed having a drink with the neighbor from time to time. Sharon said, yes, he would have a drink with her husband in life. I said, please send his love to them. I then had to laugh again at Jerry's spunky personality as I just said it as he did. I told Sharon, Your husband has a message for your niece in the room with you as well, he says, "Holy Shit, That hair color is new!" hahahahaha... Sharon and the neighbor began to laugh along with his niece. You see, we were on the phone and I surely couldn't see, but, apparently his niece has PINK hair right now hahahaha.... I said, no worries, he says he likes it ha ha.

I said to Sharon, is there a reason that he just lit a candle for me? Sharon said, I lit a candle right before we started this call!!! You see I said, Between the Pink hair reference and the candle, he is letting you know that he can see you. I was getting ready to wrap up the reading and I said, He is playing me a song from Heaven, hold on a sec so I can ask him to make it louder for me so I can hear it..... I knew the SONG!!!! I couldn't think of the name, but, I said, Let me start to sing it for you..... "So, don't ask Me Hank Why do you Drink?, Hank Why do you roll Smoke? Why Must you Live out the songs that you Wrote?"..... Sharon Screamed out "Famiy Tradition"!! YES!!!!!!!!!!!!!!! I said, he tells me he had a tattoo with a name on it as well. Sharon laughed again because her husband had a Huge Love for Hank Williams!!! Apparently the "Hank" earring he wore was for Hank as well as the tattoo he had! He loved the song Family Tradition as well and Sharon had just recently played it! It was such a Cool way to end such a Cool Reading!!! Thanks for the Laughs Jerry...

A day in the life married to a Medium? My Hubby and I were driving in the truck together after dinner tonight and I began to feel his Grandpa and Dad in Heaven join me in the truck. I said to my Husband, I am seeing Tin Snips and Wavy Tin and I feel like we are building a Tin Roof together on a Shed? My husband kept his eyes on the road as he said without missing a beat, "That is my Dad". Jim went on to say, My Dad, Friend, and I built a Tin Roof out of Corrugated Tin (Wavy Tin) on Dad's large Work Shop out back at his home. I always love learning things from Jim's Dad in Heaven about my Husband and his relationship with his Dad through validations as he joins us in Spirit. I could see the love in Jim's eyes as he recalled working on this Work Shop with his Dad and friend.

I then began to laugh at the next validation that Dad gave me as I said to Jim, Your Dad just handed me a loaf of "Wonder Bread". Jim said, "Oh Yes, Any time I went to Dad's house, he would have that Good Old White Bread that was moist and he would always offer me a sandwich on that good old "Wonder Bread" each time I went to his home.

I love it when Jim's family decides to join us in spirit and as I feel them near, I always love feeling the love of my Husband and his family as it surrounds us from Heaven.

Kristie called me this morning for her reading and I could hear the pain in her voice at the word Hello. As I began making a connection with Heaven for Kristie, I felt a Male to her side step forward. I could feel the love pouring through me for Kristie as he told me of his passing during Kristie's reading. Kristie's said, yes that is my husband Jesse. As Jesse told me about his passing, he told me that he hadn't felt good leading up to the day of his passing. He made me feel he was tired and his chest really didn't feel well. He told me that he blew off requests Kristie made for him to go get checked out by a doctor (just as most of our men do) because he was stubborn. He made me feel as though he had taken some medication in hopes of feeling better and laid down for some rest. What he showed me next in the reading took my breath away..... Jesse showed me one of his children at his side in bed when he began his journey to Heaven. He then showed me another young child of his walking in the room as well when he was passing. He showed me his beautiful wife down with him and trying to do all that she could to help him. He then showed me his Infant Son in the bassinet/crib crying as he was passing to Heaven. He showed me himself out of his body and watching all of this from a place of spirit as he continued to show me more throughout the reading. Kristie said, yes, My husband was lying in bed with our 5 year old daughter at the time that he stopped breathing. She went on to say that her Husband had a Heart related passing. Through her tears, Kristie then went on to say that their 8 year old daughter had in fact walked into the room as well when all of the commotion was going on with Jesse. Jesse said to tell his wife she had done all that she could have to save him and there truly wasn't anymore she could have done. There was a feeling I couldn't explain at first as I was getting references on my body from Jesse about his passing and that was that he was restricting my throat. As I asked him to give me more about this, I had to laugh. Jesse showed me the paramedics working on him and as he showed me this, the cuss words started flying out of my mouth as Jesse made me feel like he was laughing from Heaven. Jesse said, "I was still living when the paramedics arrived. They were treating me like I overdosed on medication! Holy Shit!!! What the Fuck were they doing with me hahaha". Kristie began to laugh through her tears as she said, "That is EXACTLY what my Husband would have said about that!!!" She said that the paramedics were trying to pump her husband's stomach (Which was why I felt my throat restricted) when in fact, he was having a Heart Attack and Kristie tried to tell the paramedics that her husband had not taken too much medication and just needed help. I loved the Feisty personality that shined through from Heaven from Jesse to Kristie. I loved that she was sensing her Husband within the words that were coming out of my mouth.

Jesse told me that his baby boy is named after him. Kristie said, yes, he is and he was only 6 months old when his Daddy passed to Heaven. Jesse then showed me a Special Teddy bear made in honor of him that was being placed with the baby. Kristie said that Jesse's sister had made a teddy bear with a tshirt that has Jesse's picture on it that she hands to the baby to play with in honor of his Daddy. Jesse put baseball caps on both of his daughter's heads in my mind's eye vision. Kristie said, my girls have been begging to get back into baseball lately and I have been thinking of putting them back into baseball because Jesse loved it when they played. I said, well, I think he supports that decision from Heaven since he is bringing it up. Jesse then showed me something that confused me. He had already told me that he has 2 daughters and 1 son in the reading, but, he was now telling me they have 4 kids, but, who am I to question spirit even if I have no Idea what it means lol. Kristie said, after my husband's passing, I took custody of our Niece. I loved that Jesse was welcoming the new addition from Heaven and letting his wife know that he didn't miss out on their niece moving in. Jesse showed me that his special rifle would be passed down to his son when he gets old enough to have it and he was so happy about this decision that Kristie made. Kristie said that she does in fact have Jesse's rifle and it will be passed down to their Son when he gets old enough to have his Daddy's Rifle.

Jesse told me that he was in the Military in life as he made me feel I needed to salute him. Kristie said, yes, he was in the military. I then said, Jesse tells me you moved 3 times together when he was in the Military and Kristie said, Yes, we moved 3 times and one of those times, we lived in Italy. Jesse said that he was given an Official Military Burial and he showed me The Folding of The Flag with this. Kristie said, yes, he was given a Military burial. He wanted his daughters to know that he got the pictures they drew for him and placed with him at his funeral. Kristie said their 5 and 8 year old daughters had colored pictures for their Daddy and placed the pictures with him in his casket. Jesse then showed me that his wife and kids were given private time with him at the funeral home after he passed. He showed me that one of his daughters kissed him on his head and he wanted her to know he got her kiss. Kristie cried as she confirmed that one daughter had kissed her Daddy on his Forehead. Jesse then showed me that Kristie held the baby within arms reach of him in that visit so that their son could touch his Daddy Goodbye. Again, through her tears, Kristie recalled holding their son close to his Daddy so that he could reach out and touch him.

Jesse said that a fundraiser was done in his honor after his passing for his family and he was so grateful for all of the people who donated to his wife and children. He said that some of his Military Buddies had donated as well and he wanted to Thank Them for stepping up for him when he couldn't be there for his family in their time of need. Kristie said that there was a Go Fund Me account set up in her honor when her husband passed and some of his Military friends did donate as well and she was very Thankful. Jesse also showed me a few of his personal friends coming to his house to help Kristie with things when she needed the help and he wanted to Thank them as well. Kristie knew of the Men Jesse spoke of and she was also grateful for their help with things since Jesse passed.

Jesse then began to tell me of Kristie's plans to honor him. He showed me that Kristie would be doing something with his boots and uniform in his honor and he loves this idea. Kristie said she was going to have a picture taken of his boots and uniform to be placed on his Headstone. Jesse showed me his shirts turning into a quilt and Kristie said she had been talking about making his shirts into a quilt for each of the kids but she wasn't sure if she could part with them just yet. Jesse then showed me teddy bears being made out of his shirts as well. Kristie was in awe that her Husband knew of so many plans as she was considering having bears made for each of the kids out of Jesse's Camo Shirts/Uniforms. Jesse then said, My Wife wears Me on her Neck. He went on to say, She wears my Wedding ring as well. Kristie said, I wear my Husband's Dog Tags on my neck and I slipped his wedding ring on the chain with the Dog Tags.

Jesse told me that he has a sister that lives out of State that he wants to send his love to. Kristie said, Yes, he does and I will send his love. Jesse then told me he has another sister who has daughters and he wants to send his love to this sister as well as his nieces. Jesse then made my heart hurt a little as he told me that another family member of his and a friend of his have not been very supportive to Kristie and her children since his passing and although he loves them, he wanted his wife to know that he is watching over this from Heaven and he sees how very difficult it has been for her. He said, "You have gone through enough with my passing and becoming a single Mom of 4 and you are doing Amazing and you don't need the extra stress". I told Kristie I would leave her with his words and Kristie said she understood and I could feel some pain release as she knew her Husband is watching over this from Heaven.

Jesse brought up signs that he sends his family and he kept showing me butterflies as he showed me the signs. Kristie said, "That is so significant because I was out back after Jesse passed and a butterfly flew right up in front of me." I interrupted Kristie and said, "He tells me he made it land on you!? Kristie's voice was filled with excitement as she carried on to say that the butterfly had in fact landed right on her hand and it stayed there for at least 10 minutes as she took pictures of it!!!!! I told her, you see, you already knew that it was your Husband that sent you that Butterfly.............

There were more validations that came through in Kristie's reading, but, I love that this Husband and Father of 4 in Heaven sent his love in the form of keeping true to his spunky personality and he gave so many current validations that his wife knows without a doubt that her Husband walks with her in life. He even showed me a large property with a pond on it that Kristie had considered moving to after his passing as a way of letting her know he house hunted with her and the kids.

At the end of the reading, Jesse said I needed to say, "I Love You, I Love you, I Love You, She said it A Million Times To Me". Kristie said that she would tell her husband over and over each day, "I Love You" and Jesse would tell her in life, "You've said it a Million times to me today". Kristie would tell Jesse, "Yes, but we never know when it is the last time we will get to say it to each other"........................ I love that Kristie left nothing unsaid..............

FARA GIBSON

Brenda was drawn as the winner of the November 1st reading give away. We did her reading yesterday afternoon and she has allowed me to share her reading as she understands the healing that lies within these stories for others. As I began to ask her loved ones to step forward for her reading, there was one loved one that stood in front of the rest. In fact, he stayed with us the whole reading and really didn't move aside for anyone else to come through which was fine by Brenda. This Special Man stepping forward for Brenda from Heaven is her Dad.

I first asked Dad to tell me how he passed. Dad made me feel as though he had numerous troubles within his body at the end of his life. Dad said that he had troubles with his Heart. In addition to the troubles with his heart, Dad showed me that he had cancer in his lungs as well as in his bladder within his body. He told me that he was very sick at the end of his life, but he said that Brenda was at his side through his journey with his illness. Brenda confirmed all of Dad's validations and she was absolutely at her Father's side through his illness. Dad then showed me Brenda holding his hand as he Journey'd to Heaven. I could hear the tears in Brenda's voice as she recalled holding her Dad's hand when he passed.

Dad told me that Brenda has 2 children that he wanted to send his love to in life. He said that she has a Son and a Daughter that he watches over from Heaven. Brenda was happy to hear Dad bring up her 2 children. Dad also wanted to send his love to his Son and wife as well from Heaven. I then got a little confused as Dad brought up 3 more children for Brenda. But, who am I to question spirit, so, I said to Brenda, he says there are 3 more children that he needs to bring up with you. Brenda's voice cracked as she said that she has 3 babies in Heaven. I told her that this was her Dad's way of letting Brenda know that her babies were safe within his arms in Heaven. I said to Brenda, do you know the Sex of those babies? Brenda said, no, I don't. I asked Dad to show me the babies and I saw 1 son and 2 daughters for Brenda in Heaven. A tearful Brenda thanked me for that information and I Thanked Dad silently in my head for the healing he had just given his daughter.

Dad told me that he had a love for the outdoors and he then showed me Deer and in his spunky sense of humor, he then handed me some Deer Jerky. Brenda said, Oh yes, Dad loved the outdoors and he loved Deer Hunting. Dad told me that he loved to fish in life as well and he showed me his Grandson fishing with him when he was young. Brenda said her son and Dad did fish together when her son was young.

I then got a reference I have never received. Dad made me feel as though he jumped on my back for a "Piggy Back Ride" and he said, My Daughter carries me on her back..... Well, this was going to be fun to describe lol..... But, as I did, Brenda knew exactly why her Dad did this. Brenda told me that she has a large tattoo in honor of her Dad since his passing and it is on her back. Dad said that Brenda has another tattoo associated with him as well. Brenda said, yes, Dad and I got a tattoo together in life once.

Dad showed me that Brenda planted a garden in his honor after his passing and he said he loves it. Brenda said, I sure did. I then said, Well, he shows me that quite a few plants didn't make it? Brenda said, I don't recall any trouble with the plants. So, I asked Dad if he could be more specific and he showed me Deer and Rabbits in the garden eating the plants. As I told Brenda about this, she laughed and said, Oh Yes!!! I lost quite a few plants to animals for sure!

Dad told me that Brenda saved some of his button down shirts. Brenda said, yes, I did. I said, He tells me you had something made out of his shirts in honor of him as well. Brenda said, Oh Wow! She went on to say that Dad's shirts had been made into a quilt in his honor!

Dad showed me a wedding coming and he wanted his daughter to know that he wouldn't be missing this wedding for the world. Brenda is getting married soon and it was a beautiful validation that this Daddy's Girl needed to Hear. Dad said, "My Daughter is wearing me to her wedding". Brenda said that she is getting a necklace to wear her Dad's ashes at her wedding so that she can include him on her special day. I told Brenda I was so proud of her for such a beautiful gesture of including her Dad on her special day. Dad said, "I brought you and your Fiance together from Heaven". Brenda and her Fiance had in fact gotten together after Dad's passing and I could feel the wonder of this Daughter for her Dad's approval lift as he said those words.

There were so many more validations in Brenda's reading, but, the biggest validation of all was LOVE and I was Blessed to share it with her! May your wedding day be Blessed Brenda.

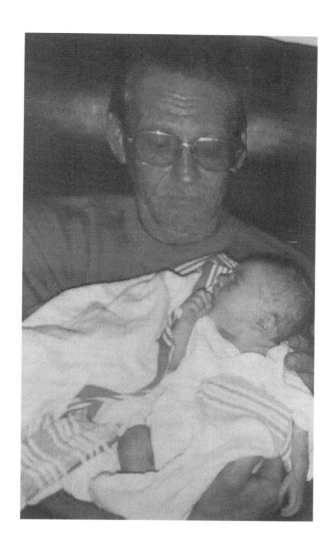

When Laura and I began her reading yesterday, she had her 10 year old daughter join us to listen in. I thought it was beautiful of Laura to be open to her daughter also hearing messages from heaven and I began to make a beautiful connection with heaven for this Mother and daughter.

As I began making my connection with heaven, I first felt a female that felt as though she was older than Laura in age and she made me feel as though she passed due to cancer. She told me that she had cancer throughout her body and she showed me that Laura and her daughter helped to take care of her at the end of her life. Laura knew exactly who this beautiful woman coming through from heaven was, she said, That is Sister.

Laura's sister in heaven showed me that Laura and her daughter are in the same home that she lived in life. Laura said that she and her daughter had just moved into her sister's home after her passing and it was beautiful than her sister knew that they were living there. Her sister told me that they had moved around the bedroom and she loves it! Laura said that she and her daughter had in fact move her sister's bedroom around and placed her sister's piano in the exact place that her sister passed to Heaven so that Laura's daughter may play the piano in a place where her aunt passed to heaven. I then said to Laura that her sister is showing me that she's placing pictures all around the walls in that bedroom. Laura said that she has taken down many beautiful pictures that her sister took of flowers and she planned to place them around on the walls in the room as well. Her sister then took me out to the back patio and made me feel as though there are 2 bird feeders out there and one was for hummingbirds and the other was for seed and that they both need to be filled. She made me feel as though she spent much time back here enjoying watching the birds come and go. Laura laughed and said that her sister absolutely loved to spend time out there watching the birds and she realized as I said this that both feeders do need to be filled and she did so and text me to let me know they were filled right after our reading lol. Her sister then showed me that Laura is now driving her car since her passing. She also showed me that Laura has hung something up in her rear view mirror area of her car that catches light like a crystal. Laura said that she had in fact decided to start driving her sister's car since her passing and that she has hung an angel from the rear view mirror in honor of her sister that is made of crystal and it catches light beautifully in her sister's honor.

Laura's sister surely wasn't going to leave out her beautiful 10 year old niece as she joined us for the reading as well. She wanted her needs to know that she says that she has worn her hats since her passing. Little Katia was pretty excited to know that her aunt can see that she wears her hats from heaven. She then told me that Katia was singing for her right before she passed to heaven and she wanted her to know that she heard her beautiful singing. I could hear Katia's tears as Laura assured her daughter that it was okay to cry. Katia's Aunt in Heaven then showed me lavender bedding for her beautiful niece. Laura said, we just got new bedding for Katia's room and it is lavender in color. Her Aunt then showed me Katia as a young girl swimming laps in her pool. Katia recalled that her aunt had taught her to swim in her pool at her home. Katia said that her aunt had made numerous videos for her just talking about life but she had forgotten to make her a video about what to do about boys? I had to laugh as I said to Katia, your aunt says to wait until you're 16! Hahaha way to go Auntie! She then showed me a balloon release that Laura and her daughter had done in her honor. She showed me that one of the balloons took off on its own and came back down and she wanted Laura and her daughter to know that she was responsible for this. Laura laughed as I brought this up and said that Katia's first balloon that she sent up came back down and popped in a tree and they had to give her another balloon to send up for her precious Aunt. We all got a good laugh that her Aunt made that balloon go a little wonky. I assured Katia that her aunt loves her very much and watches over her each and every day as well as meet her in her dreams.

Laura's sister told me that she had initially been misdiagnosed with her cancer. She made me feel as though she had fought this cancer for some time and her sister and Niece were at her side throughout her entire journey. She wanted her sister to know that she was aware that she was holding her hand as she passed to heaven. Laura's voice choked up as she found her sister knew she was at her side.

Her sister showed me the three of them boarding a boat together and made me feel as though this was significant. Laura said that her sister had held true to her promise and although she was not feeling well she's still went whale watching with she and Katia before her passing.

Her sister was been giving me a reference to a "sister saying." Laura didn't understand what this meant. It I kept getting reference to Laura having something with a "Sister Saying" on it. After our reading was complete, Laura text me a picture. With the picture, she said this..."Had to share this right away because it greeted me in a flower bed outside as I filled the bird feeders. This was at my old house and was the only outdoor decor that wasn't destroyed and thrown out. I brought it to my sisters house 2 weeks ago." With this, she sent a picture of a garden stepping stone. On the stone was a "sister saying" and it read, " Sisters are Flowers in the Same Garden"

At my Public Group Reading last week, there was a young lady sitting alone in the audience by the name of Dona. I didn't know why, but I was drawn to her from the moment she walked into the door. Her energy was amazing and the strength it took her to walk into that door alone, I knew was immeasurable, but I didn't know why I felt that way. I try not to pay attention to spirit in advance of a reading to save my energy for the connections at the time of the readings, but, about half way through the reading, I would come to understand why I felt as though Dona carried so much strength into the door with her that day.

Dona's turn came in the group reading and I felt as though I had a Male to her side coming through at her same age level. He made me feel as though his passing was sudden and unexpected. I felt as though he felt a bit off the day that he passed and had a chest/heart related passing that was unexpected. Dona knew this to be a young male that she had a relationship with earlier in life. As the reading continued, there were numerous validations that he came through with and one was that of a "Low-rider Car". As I said this validation, Dona smiled and said, oh yes, he loved Low-rider Cars in life. In fact, when the reading was over, Dona walked up to me and showed me a picture of his headstone with a "Low-rider Car" on his Headstone!!! I would say that was a pretty cool validation. But, there was something about the tattoo on Dona's shoulder that kept drawing me to her. I recall walking past her previously a few times and complimenting the beautiful tattoo. As I finished Dona's connection with this Man, I again touched her Tattoo on her shoulder and told her that I loved that she had this Memorial tattoo on her shoulder. Dona said to me, Yes, it is a Memorial Tattoo, but it is for my son and that is his Dad in Heaven that you were just connecting with as well......
I stood bewildered in the reading for a moment asking her Son to step forward, but, I felt silence. I spoke with my Spirit Guides in my Head in an instant and asked why it was that her Son's Father had come through, but not her Son. The answer was clear to me, there are some readings that are not meant to be done in a Group Environment because of the Emotional Charge that comes with them. I looked at Dona and said,

Listen to me, You and I are going to speak privately after this Group reading about your Son. We will set up a time and day for a call without charge okay? Tears fell on Dona's Cheeks as she shook her head yes and left the room temporarily to compose herself so that she could rejoin the group to witness more of the beautiful validations that were to come through for others.

Today, Dona called me for that reading. I felt a young Male coming though in her reading today that was a Son energy for Dona. He told me that he was young and that he had Passed From a rare cancer that affected his bones. Dona said that her Son Danny was only 13 years old when he passed from cancer on 07-01-2013. Danny showed me that his Mom held him in her arms as he passed to Heaven. He showed me her hand upon his chest as his heart stopped beating and told me that his Mom felt his final beat of his heart as she held him. Danny made me feel as though the number 10 and the 10th month were significant for him with his illness as well. Dona said yes, In October of 2010, when Danny was only 10 years old, he was diagnosed with Cancer. WOW..... That sure is a lot of 10's.....

Danny told me that his Mom made something in honor of him with Glitter All Over It after he passed. He laughed and said it made a mess with all of the glitter. Dona said that for Danny's first Christmas in Heaven, she decorated a small Christmas Tree to bring to his Grave and She Covered the Christmas Tree in Glitter!!! She laughed and said it truly was a mess ha ha..... Danny told me that his Mom and others in the family wear shirts in honor of him and he loves this! Dona said that Danny loved to wear shirts with silly sayings on them in life and they wear these same kind of shirts in honor of him since his passing. She said that they wore these silly shirts to his Balloon release that they held in his honor as well.

Danny said, My mom is planning another tattoo in honor of me since my passing. Dona said that she is absolutely planning a second tattoo for her son and it was beautiful that he knew of her thoughts of this as she hadn't told anyone of her plans yet. Danny showed me a Light colored Stuffed Animal with something Floppy on top of its head. I didn't recognize the kind of stuffed animal he was showing me and just kept describing it to Dona. Dona said that Danny had a stuffed Bear that he kept with him in the Hospital and Dona's Dad had taken the bear and dressed it in Scrubs with a mask on it's face and a Floppy hat on top of it's head! This was Danny's way of sending his love to his Grandpa for dressing up that Bear for him.

Danny told me that he wanted to send his love to his siblings. He showed me that his Dad's family was very important to him in life and that he spent quite a bit of time with them and wanted to send his love to them as well. Dona said, oh yes, his Dad's family was a big part of his life growing up and she knew of her Son's love for them.

Danny then placed a "Silly" hat on my head and then another one and another one. I said to Dona, he is putting Silly hats on my Head. Dona said, yes he wore silly hats all of the time since he had lost his hair with his cancer treatments. She sent pictures to me of Danny in his Silly Hats and they are Beautiful. Danny said, "Tell my Mom that I am not Swollen in Heaven anymore from my Treatments" "Tell my mom I am Cute!". Dona laughed through her tears because her Son had some swelling and water retention at the end of his life with his treatments and it was good to know that her Son felt Handsome in Heaven. Danny then made me feel like he slipped his Shoes on my feet in representation of putting them on his Mom's Feet. I laughed as he did this and told him they surely wouldn't fit me hahaha... As I gave this validation to Dona, she said that when her Son was in the hospital, his shoes would sit out in his hospital room and if she needed to quickly run out of the room to get something, she would slip Danny's shoes on her feet to run small errands in the Hospital. This was something that was private between Mother and Son and it was a beautiful validation of love. Danny made me feel as though his Mom had a significant bracelet in honor of him as well. Dona said, yes, I actually had to stop wearing it for fear that it would fall apart. She said, it is one of the rubber bracelets and it says, "Fight For Danny".

Danny then showed me something that Looked like a Wind Chime or Chandelier hanging up in honor of him. Dona knew exactly what her son was speaking of. The Hospital would give "Beads of Courage" to kids for completing different procedures like blood draws, transfusions, and dialysis.... Danny had over 500 Strands of Beads in the short amount of time he collected them and Dona made a beautiful piece of art of his beads to display them that resembles a chandelier or wind chime shape. She sent a picture of his beautiful art piece and it is amazing.

Danny told me that he loved "Hot wheel Cars" and he handed me a "Low-rider" Hot wheel car because he liked the cars his Daddy liked as well. Dona said, oh yes, he had Tons of Hot wheels and he had Low-rider cars in his collection that he loved! Danny told me that he also had a love for playing video games in life as well. Dona said, oh yes, he loved video games!

Danny took me to the Children's Hospital and told me that the staff at the Children's Hospital had signed a large Banner or sign or something large in honor of him. Dona said that The Children's Hospital had gifted her with a Large Blanket that the Nurses had signed who cared for Danny. I told her that I didn't know if she would share this with his nurses, but, if she gets the opportunity, to please send his love to them for all that they did for him and this was his way of sending his love to them from Heaven.

Danny then showed me Butterflies. He was sending lots and lots of butterflies into my vision and Dona's voice cracked with tears as she told me how significant the butterflies are. Dona went to a Butterfly Garden and while there, she was told by the facility of a beautiful belief by the local Indian Tribe and the Belief is that, You can whisper a message to a Butterfly and it will carry your message to your loved one on the other side...... Dona went on to say that part of her tattoo that couldn't be seen by me on the day of her attendance at my group reading actually has a Butterfly incorporated on her shoulder because of this beautiful belief so that she may reach over and whisper her love to her son.... On the back of her shoulder is another butterfly flying away to deliver that message... I would say that her Son has received her Messages in Heaven as he surrounded me with Butterflies to send his love to Mom........

I was so Grateful that Danny gave me that moment of silence in the reading that day. It humbled me as I realized first that each message is within Heavens control and not mine. But, it was also a beautiful reminder that the healing messages needed are always there when we need them the most. Danny was going to do things his own way from Heaven to be sure his Mom got some private time with me. I'd say, that was just fine by me.

There was a woman named Sarah at my Public Group reading last weekend that received messages from her loved ones in Heaven as her Husband sat next to her in the audience. When the group reading was complete, I knew she had received healing messages within the reading, but, I felt that she needed more. I told Sarah to please call me for a one on one phone call without charge and we set up a date. Today, was the day that we did her reading. Prior to Sarah calling, I saw a flash in my vision of a Stuffed Frog toy. I had no idea why I saw the stuffed frog, but, it would be something worth mentioning in our reading because the flash was so vivid.

When Sarah called me for her reading, I mentioned that I had seen a flash of a Frog prior to her calling me, and I continued to give her my opening speech. As I began to make the connections with Heaven, I first felt as though I had a Female Sister energy coming though that made me feel as though her passing was head related. She made me feel as though she was sick at the end of her life. Sarah said, yes, that is my Husband's sister, June. June made me feel as though someone has a small tattoo in her honor that she loves very much. Sarah said that her Husband's daughter has a little tattoo in honor of her Aunt who is in Heaven. As I connected with Sarah's Sister in Law, I again saw a flash of a Green Frog Stuffed Animal and I said to Sarah, "I don't know why she keeps showing this to me, but she showed me a Frog Stuffed Animal before we started your reading and she is showing it to me again and it is green." Sarah laughed as she said, "Yes, it is Green with black spots and I am Holding the frog right now in my hand because my Sister in Law in Heaven gave it to me before she passed." I can tell you that at that moment, I was covered in Goosebumps at such a beautiful validation of love and that her Sister in Law in Heaven still sees and watches over Sarah as well. Sarah's Sister in Law June also had someone very special with her in Heaven. June had another young female in Heaven with her.

As I began to ask the young female of her passing, she told me that her passing was sudden or unexpected. She made me feel as though she was to the side of Sarah which for me is within the same age group. Sarah said, Yes, that is my Sister, Pam. Pam showed me herself in a car with a vehicle coming straight at her side of the car. She said that a Man was driving the other vehicle that hit her and she passed instantly to Heaven. Sarah's tears as she confirmed that her sister had passed in a vehicle accident where she was T-boned on Pam's side of the vehicle by a male driver could be heard through the phone. Pam told me that the man who hit her had answered and payed for his mistake in hitting her. Sarah said, Yes, he did answer for hitting my sister.

Pam told me to tell Sarah, "I Pinky Swear"……. Sarah broke down in tears the moment that I said this. She said that when Pam Passed to Heaven, she had told a "Pinky Swear" to her sister and no one would have known of this. Pam placed a Beautiful Rosary around my neck and made me feel as though she has this Rosary in Heaven. Sarah said, yes, we buried her with a Rosary on her neck. Pam then told me that she also has the small stuffed animal in Heaven that was placed with her as well at her funeral. Sarah said that they had placed a little stuffed animal with Pam from her Son that she left behind in life. Pam made me feel as though I was dressed in lace. As I described this to Sarah, she told me that her sister Pam had been buried in a lace dress. I said to Sarah, "I love that your sister is giving me validations that there is no way that I would know if she wasn't a part of this beautiful conversation." I then said to Sarah, "Your sister tells me that you moved her hair over to the side in the casket." Sarah's tears began to hit the phone as she said, Yes, I pushed her bangs over to the side! I told Sarah, Your Sister says, Thanks! (It truly wasn't about her hair being out of place in her casket, but more of Pam's way of letting her sister Sarah know that she was with her and watching over her during that difficult time from Heaven.

Pam told me that she and the family had just moved before she passed. She showed me that she lived with her Mom. Sarah said that this was true. Pam wanted to send her love to her Mom and she showed me a ring slipping on the finger of Mom. Sarah said that Mom has a ring of Pam's and she wore it since her sister's passing. Pam showed me that her Sister has a small tattoo in honor of her and said that a few others have tattoos as well that she wanted to send her love to. Sarah said that her Mom and Sister both have tattoos in honor of Pam and she would pass along her love.

Pam told me that Sarah is going on a trip out of State soon and she wanted her sister to know that she will be going on this trip with her from Heaven. Sarah laughed through her tears as she said, Yes, we are planning a trip to Disney Land. I said, well, your Sister will be going on that trip with you.

Pam then showed me a flash of a picture of she and her sister Sarah and I described what I was seeing to Sarah. I said, well, I don't know what this is, but I will describe it..... Your sister is showing me the 2 of you dressed up and your faces are white or really light in the picture and your hair is all Ratty also? Sarah knew the picture that her sister spoke of and said, yes, there is a picture of Pam and I in Prom Dresses at Halloween with our faces painted white and we had Ratty Hair, we were Dead Prom Dates hahahaha..... I told Sarah I would love to see the picture and she said she would love to find the picture as well.

Pam showed me metal and a welding reference and although I thought it was an odd reference, who am I to judge lol..... As I reluctantly told Sarah what I was seeing, she said, Yes, Pam worked at a Steel Company! Oh Cool I said cause I almost didn't say it lolololol.

Pam wanted her sister Sarah to know that they had typical sister issues in life, but that all of that is water under the bridge now. She wanted Sarah to know how very much she loves her as she watches over her from Heaven. Pam told me that she had brought Sarah and her Husband together from Heaven. Those were the words that Sarah had waited so long to hear so that she could let go of the pain she carried for the last 9 years since her Sister passed. I told Sarah that her Sister hadn't come through in the Group Environment at the Reading because she knew she would be able to push me from Heaven to do this more privately for Sarah and that was exactly what Sarah needed. It was a beautiful reunion between 2 Sisters and a Sister in Law who came through long enough to send her love in the form of a Frog!

There are times that I feel compelled to give a reading to a person or family as I know it will be life changing. I know that each of us has losses and each of us would love a reading. I sometimes wish I could clone myself because there is truly no way I could keep up with the amount of requests I get behind the scenes. But, as I read Brittany's message, there wasn't a spot on my face that was dry from tears. I couldn't imagine on a human level going through all that she and her family had been through, though on a spirit level, it all made perfect sense and I wondered if I could help Brittany and her family make sense of all that happened with the help of Heaven. Brittany has allowed me to share her story because today I reached out to her and asked her if she had time to speak with me. Needless to say, Brittany made time and that phone call was precious. There were parts about Brittany's story that I knew in advance of this reading because she had written about it to me in her story. Those of you that know me, are aware that I don't want to know anything up front so that you can be assured that your loved one is giving me these validations with no prior knowledge. So, I told Brittany as we started her reading that I would be asking her Brother in Heaven for more than she gave me and extra validations that there would be no way I would know without his help from Heaven. Brittany understood and we began.

Brittany's Brother Richie in Heaven began to step forward in our reading. Richie told me that he and his Dad had trouble more than once in life. Brittany said, yes they did. Richie showed me that he told his Sister to leave the house that day because he needed to protect her from their Dad. Brittany said, yes, Richie asked Mom and I to leave and take my boyfriend and his brother home because no one needed to see Dad acting so angry that day. Brittany had told me in the story that her Father had gotten into an argument with her Mom. Brittany tried to ask her Dad to please stop yelling at her Mom. Brittany never expected what would happen next that day as she tried to help her Mom. Her brother Richie intervened in the argument and redirected Dad's attention at himself to save his Mom and Sister that day. Richie told his sister to leave and an argument ensued between her brother and Dad. As they loaded Brittany's

HEAVEN IS WITHIN US

boyfriend in the car that day, they saw a physical altercation ensuing with Dad and Richie because Dad got Physical. She saw her Brother get back up after Dad caused him to fall down the stairs outside and he picked up an item to defend himself from Dad. Her Brother broke free from Dad and as he was in the process of running for his life, Richie's Dad shot his own son in the back with a Shotgun. Mom and Brittany were pulling back into the driveway and the yard was filled with police and fire vehicles. Brittany made it to her brother and knew that he was in Heaven. The rest of the story would come from Richie.......

Richie told me that his Dad did not get away with taking his life. He showed me that his Dad was arrested and sentenced to Jail time. Brittany said, yes, our Dad was sentenced to 20 years in Prison for Richie's passing. I then asked Richie to give me loving validations for his sister. The first thing he showed me was an item that his sister had hung from her rear view mirror in his honor. Brittany began to cry as I gave her this validation as she said, YES! Richie told me that his Sister and others have tattoos in honor of him. Brittany said, yes my brother and I have tattoos for Richie. I said, he tells me that someone has a tattoo on their arm for him as well. Richie then showed me a ribbon with his name written on it. Brittany said that she has another living brother who had a tattoo that matched Richie's tattoo on his arm and after his passing, her brother went back to the tattoo parlor and had a ribbon with Richie's name on it added to the tattoo.

Richie told me that he loved 4 wheeling and mudding in life. Brittany said, yes, he loved to go 4 wheeling. He wanted his sister to know that he sees that she is wearing one of his shirts while we are on the phone together. Brittany laughed through her tears as she said that she did in fact have one of her brother's shirts on while we were speaking. I told her that this was her brother's way of letting her know that he still sees her from Heaven.

Richie wanted his sister to know that he had not missed out on her children from Heaven. He said to tell her that he knows that Brittany named her first daughter after him. Brittany had given her Brother's name to her first born

109

daughter. Richie then showed me that Brittany has a little boy as well who is a little cowboy and Richie told me that Brittany named him after his Daddy. Brittany said, yes, we have a little boy and he dresses in Jeans and boots and he is named after my Husband, his Daddy. Richie told me that Brittany has 3 children. He said she has 2 girls and a little boy and he watches over all of them from Heaven. Richie later told me that Brittany's Husband was with her today as we were talking. Brittany said, yes, my Husband is here. Richie said, Her husband is the same boyfriend she had on the day that he passed to Heaven that she had to take home that day. He wanted Brittany to know that he hadn't missed out on their wedding day. He showed me Mom at the wedding and his Brother stepping into the shoes of Dad there to support her. Brittany said that she had a small court house wedding and that her Mom and Brother were there. I assured her that her Brother in Heaven didn't miss her wedding for the world.

At this point in the reading, I had to tell Brittany the most important words that he needed her to hear. Richie said that "I would have defended my family a million times again even if it ended up the same way". He went on to tell me, " I saved Mom's life that day and Dad would have taken Mom's life if I hadn't been there to save her." He told me to remind Brittany, "I told you to leave that day and there is no need for you to carry guilt for leaving. It wouldn't have changed the outcome if you had stayed". He wanted his Mom and family to live life to it's fullest potential knowing he is at their side from Heaven.

He told me that he needed to send his love to Mom. He said Mom wears a necklace for him. Brittany said, Yes she does and I will send his love to her. Richie told me that he sends birds as well as messes with electronics as signs he is around. He then gave me a validation of hiding keys on his sister as well and then putting them right back near where they belonged in the the first place. Brittany laughed and said Oh Wow, just 2 days ago, I lost my keys!! She said, I knew exactly where I had placed them and I looked everywhere for my keys!!! She said, after looking everywhere, I found them in the garbage can that was sitting next to where

I placed them and I thought to myself, "What in the world?" hahaha-haha.... That my Dear is your Mischievous Brother in Heaven that Loves you very much.... He protected you that day and will look out for you from Heaven until you meet again some day............ I got a note from Brittany after her surprise reading and it said just enough to make me cry again.......

"I just wanted to Thank You So Much for blessing us with that. You don't know how much that meant to us. I've longed to know for so long. You really helped heal my soul I'm forever grateful for everything you did for my family. And I would love for you to write something, you always word everthing so beautifully. You're an amazing woman Thank You Again......"

Last week, an anonymous Man paid for a reading to be gifted on this page to someone in need. Yesterday, I did the reading for the young lady named Toni that was the recipient of that reading. The amount of Healing that came with that Gift for Toni and her family was priceless.

As I began Toni's reading, I first had her Mom coming through from Heaven. Mom told me that she was sick for some time and that she had lung/breathing issues as well as she gave me a reference to having had cancer. Toni said, they had wondered if Mom had cancer. Mom said that she never wanted to be a burden on her family and so if they asked how her health was, she would change the subject. Toni said that this is exactly how Mom was in life and I told Toni that Mom did it her way and that she loves them all so much. Mom then told me that she needs to send her love to her 3 boys here with Toni. Mom then told me that she has her 4th son in Heaven with her. Toni said, I have a brother in Heaven with Mom and she does have 3 sons still living. At this point in the reading, Toni's brother began to give validations as well, but, for the sake of keeping this less confusing, we will continue to speak of Mom first. Mom then told me, "One Of My Boys Is There With Toni Right Now!" As I asked Toni if her Brother was with us listening to the reading, Toni said, Yes he is, he just arrived as we were starting the reading!!! My Heart shined a bit as Mom made sure to let her Boy know that she knew he was joining us for this reading. Mom then told me that another one of her Sons was going to join us for this reading today but he had changed his mind and didn't come because he didn't believe in Mediums. But, she wanted him to know she loves him even though he didn't come ha ha.... Toni said, WOW, that is exactly right! One more of my Brothers was going to come and changed his mind because he didn't think this was real. I said, Yeah, well, Mom is giving him a little laugh from Heaven ha ha and she sends her love.

Mom told me that the "Angels On You" reference was from her. Toni said, yes that the tattoo on her arm that reads "Angels On You" that she used a picture of in the inspirational quote she posted for the give-away was a saying that her Mom used in life as she grew up and she has since tattooed it on herself in honor of Mom. Mom was then giving me a reference to Handing Down Ceramic items of hers to someone important in the family. Toni said that just two days ago, she had passed down her Mom's Ceramic Art pieces to her daughter so that she could paint them like her Grandma in Heaven did. This was Mom's way of letting Toni know that she is not missing out on that precious granddaughter from Heaven. Mom then showed me paintings of landscapes in frames that she had gifted them as well. Toni said that they did in fact have paintings that Mom had Given them in life of landscapes that are in Frames.

I then said to Toni, She just interrupted what she was showing me and she placed a ring on your finger and says you have her ring. Toni began to cry as I said this. Toni went on to say that she had JUST asked her Mom in her head to please bring up the Ring that she wears of Mom's. Toni said at the moment that she finished silently asking Mom in her head to bring the ring up was when I gave her the validation from Mom. That Moment was a Moment that Toni will never forget, for it was the moment that she realized herself that her Mom still hears her from Heaven.

Mom told me that her children have she and her Son's ashes next to one another. Mom went on to tell me that someone in the family is going to mix some of her ashes with her Son's ashes in honor of them. Toni said, yes, one of my brothers was going to mix my brother's ashes with Mom's in a necklace. I told her that Mom loves this idea. I then said, Mom says you are thinking of burying their ashes and she wants you to know that you don't need to spend that kind of money on them. Toni and her brother laughed and Toni's brother said that Mom never wanted them to spend a bunch of money on her in life and so it was fitting to hear that from Mom from Heaven as well. Mom wanted to send her love to all of her grandchildren as well. I then received validations from her Son in Heaven who was at her side.

I told Toni that her Brother was coming through from Heaven and assured her that her Brother and Mom are together in Heaven. Toni cried as she heard this because it was something that she hoped she would hear in her reading without having to ask. Her brother told me that his passing was sudden and unexpected. Toni said, yes, it was. He told me that he and his brother who was listening in with Toni sure were trouble together ha ha..... When you get a validation like that, you ask for a good story with it, so I asked Toni's Brother in Heaven to give me more. He showed me he and his brother getting into a fight with some others and showed me that his brother was arrested for this good old fashioned brotherly tiff. His brother on the phone with me laughed and said that he and his brother had in fact gotten into a fight and he had in fact been arrested for that ha ha.. Oh Boy.... Boys will be boys......

Her brother in Heaven told me that he left behind a daughter in life and he wanted to send his love to her. Toni said that her Brother does have a little girl. He then showed me a certificate she was just given in school. Toni said, yes, she is only 3 and she got a certificate for reading just recently! Daddy isn't missing out on his little girl from Heaven.

I then said to Toni, Your brother is showing me an older white car and he tells me that you all had to share it? Toni and her Brother listening in started to laugh at the memory of that car. Her brother in Heaven then told me that they were supposed to rotate who's night it was to drive the car, but that none of them shared it very well as teens hahahahaha..... Toni laughed again as she said, that he was so right hahahahaha....

Her brother showed me that there were tattoos in his honor and he loves them. He also said that there was a significant tattoo on his brothers arm associated with him as well. Toni said that numerous people had gotten tattoos in honor of her brother and that one of her brothers has a tattoo that was the same as his on his arm.

I told Toni that her brother was showing me a large black dog with him in Heaven. Toni said, yes, we had a family dog that was a Black Lab that passed. I then laughed as her brother said, "Tell her I have the Little Shit Dog Too" Toni and her brother on the phone began to laugh and Toni said that as soon as I brought up the Lab, she had written on the paper in front of her that she wondered if the little dog was with him in Heaven too. Toni said that the little dog was also a family dog that her brother had fallen in love with and he would refer to it as a "Little Shit" all the time and it became his dog before it passed. It was good to know that their dogs are in Heaven with Mom and their brother.

Her brother and Mom did a beautiful job bringing love and validations that they are watching over Toni and her family from Heaven. (Even if they don't believe in Mediums and decide not to come he he he) None of this would have been possible for Toni and her family if it hadn't been for one Anonymous Man who decided to be an Earth Angel for someone on this page. Thank You Earth Angel...........................

A Mother named Stephanie reached out to me out of desperation last weekend. The email that she sent to me took my breath away. Stephanie's 2 year old Son Brantlee passed to Heaven in a Tragic Accident just 2 weeks ago when he was struck by his Mommy's car. I couldn't reach out to Stephanie the day that I got her email because I was headed out of town with my family. Her email weighed Heavy on my mind for days. Yesterday, I asked God, "Is She Ready for a Reading God? If she is Ready to hear from her little boy so soon, please send him to me now to give me a validation that only she would know God." As soon as I asked this, I felt Stephanie's little boy step forward from Heaven. He kept showing me his little hand on mine over and over he showed me his little hand on mine. I asked him why he was showing me this? He told me that his Mommy had done something Special with his little hand on hers after his passing. This was what I had asked for from God and Stephanie's Son and so I reached out. I responded back to Stephanie in a message that read, "I have a question and it may seem random, but there is a reason behind it. Did you do something with your son's hands or hand prints after his passing?"................. Stephanie responded, "I took pictures of mine and his hands holding while he laid in his casket".................... I knew in that moment that I had to speak with Stephanie with no charge.....

Late last night, I messaged Stephanie and asked her if she could speak with me and she said that she hasn't been sleeping and would love to speak to me. As I began Stephanie's reading, little Brantlee made me feel as though his head and chest were affected in an accident. I could hear the tears in Stephanie's voice as she said, Yes Mam. Brantlee then told me the words that his Mommy needed to hear, He said, my Mommy thought I was with someone else that day that was going to watch me. He said, but the girl that was going to watch me thought that I was with my Mommy. He said, my Dad thought I was with Mom, and Mom thought the other person had me. Brantlee said, "Everyone just lost track for a moment who I was with and I was playing with the car and fixing it like a big boy near the tires of the car". He then said, Please tell my

Mommy that I didn't suffer when she pulled her car out that day and I went straight to Heaven. Stephanie desperately needed to know that her little boy knew that this was an accident and before she could even ask if he knew, he had given his Mommy the words that her heart needed for he knew that she never intended the accident that day. Brantlee showed me that his Mommy and Daddy were both trying to help him after the accident and he wanted them to take what they saw that day and please hand those memories to God because he is perfect now in Heaven.

Brantlee then began to tell me about his Daddy in the reading. He showed me that his Daddy loves the outdoors. He gave me an offroading reference for his Daddy. Stephanie giggled through her tears and said, yes, his Daddy loves the outdoors. I said to Stephanie, Is his Daddy there with you? Stephanie said, Yes, his Daddy is right her listening. I just kind of smiled to myself because that was why little Brantlee had begun to tell me about his Daddy and I didn't know that Daddy was with us on the call. Brantlee told me that he loved getting wrenches from his Daddy and working on the quads and stuff in the garage with his Daddy. He said, "Daddy and I are Buddies". Brantlee then told me that he shares a name with his Daddy also. Stephanie said, yes, he and his Daddy have the same middle name. He told me that Daddy works hard for their family away from the home and he showed me callused hands on his Daddy. Brantlee's Daddy said that he does work long days away from home and he does work with his hands. I reminded Brantlee's Dad how much his little boy loves him.

Brantlee showed me that there was a group of people that did a balloon release in his honor after his passing. Stephanie said, yes we did a balloon release. I told Stephanie that he wanted everyone to know that he got the notes they wrote on the balloons from Heaven as he showed me White Balloons. Stephanie said, we did use white balloons and we wrote notes to Brantlee on the balloons. Brantlee then told me that his Mommy saved some of his hair after he passed. Stephanie said, yes, I had a lock of his hair clipped to save after he passed.

Brantlee told me that he is his Mommy and Daddy's 1st child and he loved how spoiled he was in life. Stephanie said, oh yes, that boy was spoiled. He wanted his Mommy and Daddy to know that he has the stuffed animal with him in Heaven that was placed in his casket with him at the funeral. Stephanie said, yes, my Dad had bought him a stuffed monkey before he passed and when he passed, my Dad placed the monkey in the casket with Brantlee.

Brantlee said that Mommy wears a necklace in honor of him and Stephanie said that she had been gifted a necklace in honor of her Son's passing that she wears. I told her to send his love to the woman that gave her the necklace as well. Brantlee then told me that a female is planning a tattoo on her arm in honor of him and he said he used to visit this girl all of the time and please send his love to her for thinking of him with the tattoo. Stephanie said that she has a close friend that is planning an arm tattoo for Brantlee and she works at a local store that she and Brantlee would go to and visit her all of the time.

Brantlee then told me that we would go to a house with a little girl the same age as him and they would play together. He said, "This was an arranged marriage" hahaha.... Stephanie laughed because they do have friends they would visit who have a little girl Brantlee's age and the parents would always joke that they were going to be boyfriend and girlfriend when they got bigger.

Little Brantlee then showed me himself jumping on a little trampoline, boing, boing, boing..... He told me he loved it. Stephanie said that her Mom had a little trampoline that their son loved to play on from time to time. Brantlee said that his Mommy had a picture blown up really big of him. Stephanie said, Yes, I just had a picture blown up of his.

Brantlee said that someone has a home full of plants and flowers in honor of him. He said that the plants and flowers are everywhere and they are beautiful. He made me feel as though they were gifts from his passing and he loved each and every person that sent them. Stephanie said, yes, the plants and flowers are at his Grandparent's home on his Daddy's side right now and they are tending to them for Brantlee.

Brantlee said that the community really came together in honor of him when he passed and he loves them all so much. He said there were fundraisers done for him and he was thankful. He then showed me another Fundraiser and showed me cars with it. Stephanie said, yes, there is a fundraiser coming next weekend that is a drag race and Brantlee loved cars in life! I told her that her little boy will be at that Fundraiser.

How do you let 2 parents know that their only son and child is perfect in Heaven? How do you explain to them how amazingly beautiful their son is to have reached his Soul's growth at such a young age that he was intended to graduate at such a young age to the next part of his Soul's amazing Journey with God. How do you tell these parents that their Son blessed them with more strength in his passing than they ever knew was possible to carry and within that blessing lies their own soul's growth. How do you help them to see that by carrying their son with them in all that they do in life, then they are not living without him....... This is my life's path.... This is my journey..... How you ask? You just have to be as honest as you can while sharing Heaven and know that you have a team of Angels standing behind you when you do...

I had a woman named Camille reach out to me this weekend because she needed an emergency reading. Camille called me on Sunday for her emergency reading and she has allowed me to share her reading with each of you.

As I began Camille's reading, I had a young female stepping forward from heaven and she said, this is my mommy on the phone with you. I asked Camille if she has a daughter in heaven and she said yes, my daughter Baylee.

As I begin to ask Baylee about her passing, she told me that her passing was sudden and unexpected. She told me that she got an infection in her lungs that caused her passing. Baylee showed me that she got pneumonia and the pneumonia caused her passing. Baylee told me that her mom did everything she could to keep her healthy. She told me that mommy took her to the hospital. She said, they knew me at the hospital. Baylee then showed me herself kicking a wheelchair and she said, I don't need my wheelchair in heaven anymore Mommy. Baylee went on to tell me that the anniversary of her passing was on this day that we were speaking. She also told me that from the time she got sick until the time that she passed, it was only a week's time. Camille said that the anniversary of her daughter's passing was in fact on the same day we were doing her reading. Camille said that her daughter was in a wheelchair throughout her life and that they absolutely knew her at the hospital. Camille went on to say that her daughter came down with pneumonia and though the hospital gave it their best efforts, Baylee passed to Heaven due to her pneumonia within one week's time. Baylee told me that her Mommy held her in her arms as she went to Heaven. Baylee said, my Daddy was there too and he held my hand while I went to Heaven. Camille said, yes I was laying in bed with my arms around Baylee when she passed and her Daddy was there at her side as well.

Baylee wanted to talk about her sisters. She told me that her sisters are in school and now and this is new for them. She said the girls are starting to read and she is very proud of them. She told me that her sisters are coloring pictures in honor of her and that mommy has pictures that her sisters Drew and painted hanging on the fridge for her. Camille said yes, her twin sisters started preschool and they are starting to read. She said that her sisters color and paint pictures in honor of Baylee often and they are in fact hanging on the refrigerator.

Baylee gave me a reference to mommy having her hair done and doing something with her hair. Camille said that Baylee loved to go to the hair salon and have her hair done and she said she had a great time listening to all of the salon chatter from the other women in the room.

Baylee told me that her mommy and daddy are no longer together in life but that she loves them both very much. She said, my Daddy has a wife and I need to send my love to her as well because she was a very good second Mommy to me. Camille understood this very well and told me that she is actually really good friends with Baylee's second Mommy. Camille said that she was very good to her daughter and she always appreciated her as well.

Baylee then told me that Camille is remarried as well and she wants to please send her love to her second daddy as well. She told me that her second daddy work very hard so that mommy could spend time with her when she needed her the most and she wanted to thank him for all he did. Camille said yes, he was working and taking care of our twins around the clock so that I could stay with Baylee in the hospital and she assured me that these words would mean so much to her husband.

Baylee told me that she wasn't able to speak in life and she said, I'm chatting now haha. Camille said yes, my daughter was unable to speak in life and this is just beautiful. Baylee told me that the family put some of her ashes in the flowers in the dirt outside and she loves this. She also showed me that there is a pinwheel in the garden in honor of her and she loves this is well. Camille said wow, we have a flower garden that we made in honor of Baylee and we sprinkled some of her ashes in the garden. She said, I just put a pinwheel out there just days ago! This was her beautiful daughter's way of letting her know that she sees the beautiful way that mommy has honored her

Baylee went on to tell me that her name is on a brick in honor of her and that this brick is next to a tree. Camille said yes, the school honored her with a brick and it is next to a tree. Baylee sad, please tell my mommy that I loved taking the bus to school! Camille laughed as I said these words because she said it was so hard for her to watch Baylee Drive Away on the school bus and she always wondered if she liked it or not!

Baylee said, my Mommy has pictures of me with flowers around them. She said, please tell Daddy thank you for the flowers. Camille said wow, my ex-husband is moving and he just recently gave me some flowers from Baylee's room in his home and I just set the flowers up around her picture in my home! This was Baylee's way of letting her daddy know that she saw the gesture of him giving her flowers to Mommy as well as letting mommy know that she sees how she has them set up in her home in honor of her.

Baylee told me that she and her family went to Sea World and life and she made me feel as though it was the trip of a lifetime. She told me that her family also went to SeaWorld in honor of her after she passed and she wanted them to know that she was with them on this beautiful trip. Camille said yes, Baylee took a trip with my ex-husband and I to SeaWorld when we were still married and it was a trip of a lifetime for her. Camille went on to say that she and her family also went on a trip to SeaWorld in honor of her after she passed, just as she said.

Baylee told me that she has a brother as well and she wanted to please send her love to him. She said that she and her brother have the same dad in life. She told me that her brother enjoys skateboarding. Camille said yes, she does have a brother that shares the same father as her and, he loves to skateboard. Baylee told me that her brother's grades started dropping after she passed to Heaven and she wanted her brother to know how proud she is of him that he brought his grades back up. Camille said yes, my son's grades did drop when his sister passed because he had such a hard time with her passing but he has really worked hard to bring them back up.

Baylee wanted to thank her family for helping another child with her wheelchair. She said, thank you so much forgiving my wheelchair to another child who needed it. She said, I'm so glad you didn't just sit and stare at it mommy. Camille laughed as I said this because she really truly just wanted to sit in front of her daughter's chair and stare at it each day but she knew how much it would help another child and so she did donate it to help another family in need. It was beautiful to hear her daughter's encouraging words.

There were so many more validations that came through from Baylee for her entire family. The love between this mother and daughter was undeniable and beautiful. Baylee's unconditional love for her entire family made me smile from ear-to-ear. They way that Camille, her husband and family share love for Baylee with her Ex husband and his wife so freely was very humbling and refreshing to witness. Baylee is blessed by her family. Baylee's family is grateful for her blessings of pure and unconditional love in their life's as well.

I didn't expect to receive such a beautiful testimonial after Camille's reading. It put a light in my soul!

" Thank you again for the emergency reading-I was so nervous and could barely speak and really just wanted to hold onto that space with you and her. I will try to wait but I will do this again-it means so much to know she is here with us and can see what we do. You are just amazing to share your time and talent with those of us who have lost loved ones.... especially children because it is so hard to go on as a Mama without your baby. So much love and light to you and your family. -till next time, Camille"

Last night, I did a reading for a woman named Jennifer. Jennifer had been referred to me buy a close friend of mine named Jolene. Jolene knew the healing that could happen in a reading for Jennifer and so she sent her my way. Little did Jennifer or I know that we have a connection ourselves. That connection came through loud and clear during Jennifer's reading. She has allowed me to share her story with all of you.

When Jennifer called me, I told her that I have a male above her who makes me feel as though he is her dad. He made me feel as though he was sick at the end of his life with cancer and he made me feel as though his passing was chest/heart related. Jennifer said yes, my dad did have cancer and he never told anyone and his passing was chest related because he had passed from heart attack while on the golf course.

Dad made me feel as though I should salute him and he told me that he fought in Vietnam for our country. Jennifer said yes, my dad did fight in Vietnam and he was buried with honors. Dad told me that he was exposed to Agent Orange in Vietnam and this is what brought upon his cancer. Jennifer said yes, my dad was exposed to agent orange and we actually got a memo about his exposure after his passing.

Dad told me that Jennifer is planning to get a tattoo in honor of him on her skin. Jennifer said yes, I am planning a tattoo in honor of Dad. Dad said, my daughter is getting this tattoo on her wrist. Jennifer said yes that is exactly where I'm getting it. Dad said his name would be included in this tattoo and Jennifer said yes, I'm getting my dad's last name tattooed on my wrist.

Dad told me that he has multiple daughters and he wanted to send his love to each of them. He made me feel as though three of his daughters are different than the others and Jennifer said yes, there is quite an age gap between three of us and the others. Dad told me that his daughters wear bracelets in honor of him and he wanted to thank them for this. He told me that one of the bracelets broke at the clasp. At the time of our reading, Jennifer was unsure if one of the clasps had broken on one of her sisters bracelets. After our reading, Jennifer had talked to her mom and found out that her sisters bracelet had indeed broken at the clasp and it was something that Jennifer herself wasn't even aware of at the time of the reading. I love it when spirit gives me validations like that because when the client doesn't even know the answer to a validation then it is beautiful proof that heaven knows so much more than we do and our loved ones don't miss even the smallest details.

Dad told me that at the time of his passing he was in a relationship with a woman that he loves very much in life. He made me feel as though they were not married but he also made me feel as though she deserved a marriage from him because of the love they had in life. Jennifer understood this well because she knew how much her dad loved this woman.

Dad was then telling me that although he and Mom were no longer together in life that he wanted to send his love to her as well. He said, please tell Mom that I realized I could have been a better husband and father if I had drank a little less in life. Jennifer agreed that her dad did enjoy his drinking in life and she would pass the message of Love on to Mom. Dad told me that Jennifer's mom was recently having some health issues and he wanted to her to know that he was watching over this from Heaven. Jennifer said yes, my mom has had some health issues recently and she is stubborn as my dad was in taking care of them. Dad was showing me an engraved ring for Jennifer's mom and he wanted to thank Jennifer for this ring. Jennifer gasped as I said this and she said oh wow, he's talking about the ring that I purchase for my mom and I had it engraved with my mom and dads information on the ring with both of their birthstones. It was beautiful to know that Dad knew of this gift that Jennifer had given to her mom in honor of Dad.

Dad told me that he loved to fish in life and he made me feel as though this is something that he and Jennifer did as father and daughter together. Jennifer said, oh yes, my Dad loved to fish and we absolutely fished together. Dad said, my girl baited her own hook. Jennifer said yes I did because he taught me how. Dad was showing me that there are pictures of Jennifer when she was young with a baseball cap on and dad was standing in the picture. Jennifer said yes, I played baseball when I was a kid and my dad was the coach and there are pictures of me in my ball cap with Dad in the picture. Dad then said, there were two coaches LOL and he made me feel as though there was a joke there. Jennifer began to laugh because she remember that dad was the head coach and spent a lot of time studying and really placing his focus on making the kids great and the second coach would just kind of show up for the games and they used to laugh about this.

Dad wanted to reference another ring and say thank you to Jennifer for this ring that she had purchased for him. Jennifer said, I bought my dad a ring and I was supposed to see Dad within days of his passing so I could give it to him and I never had an opportunity to give him the ring so I still have it. Jennifer said, I even wanted him buried with it which didn't happen. I told Jennifer that Dad was aware of her beautiful gift from heaven and he wanted to thank her for the ring.

I said to Jennifer, what's with the puppy? Your dad's showing me a puppy in heaven. Jennifer again was in awe because her dog just recently had a litter of puppies and one of the puppies had passed and she said that she made mention out loud to her dad in heaven to please keep the puppy safe with him. This was Dad's way of answering Jennifer's request. Dad told me that the puppy was a runt and had found its way under the blanket where the puppy's mama had sat on it. Jennifer said wow, that's exactly right. I assured her that her puppy is in good hands in heaven.

Dad told me that his daughter just bought a new car and he wanted her to know how very proud of her she is. Jennifer said yes, I just got my dream car, a Mercedes Benz. Dad told me that the car needs new tires and Jennifer laughed and said yes, it does need new tires, but otherwise it is perfect!

Dad told me that his daughter is a business owner and he wanted her to know that he has seen her beautiful progress in life and he is so very proud of her. Jennifer said that she and her husband started the business just before Dad's passing but they hadn't had an opportunity to tell him about it because they were going to surprise him. It was beautiful to know that dad's sees she and her husband's business. Dad told me that she and her husband had started the business at home and have since bought a piece of property for their business to grow it. Jennifer said yes, we have a salvage business and it did start at our home and we have grown and purchased a property for our business.

I told you at the beginning of this story that Jennifer and I had a connection. You see, when Jennifer was brought to my page by Jolene, and she read a story that I shared about my friend and brother Kenny who passed in a motorcycle accident, she realized that the Kenny I was speaking of in my story, was the same Kenny that she had dated years ago and she didn't know that he had passed. Jennifer had previously reached out to me for the details of Kenny's passing, but as we began our reading last night, I hadn't put together that I was speaking to the same Jennifer. Last night in Jennifer's reading, Kenny came through for Jennifer!

As Kenny came through, he told me that Jennifer didn't have any kids when they were together. Jennifer said yes, I had my children after Kenny and I dated. Kenny told me that he had fixed Jennifer's car for her. Jennifer said yes, that's actually how we met. Kenny was a motorcycle mechanic and he could fix just about anything with just little crazy things that you could almost pick up off the floor and he was showing me little trinkets from the shop like this and telling me that Jennifer had some of them saved. Jennifer said oh my gosh, I have the stupid bolts that he handed me after fixing my car saved in my Hope

Chest! Kenny told me that Jennifer had a tooth issue when the two of them were together and he laughed as he showed me that he put epoxy on it. Jennifer said oh wow!!! Jennifer said that when she and Kenny were together that she chipped or broke a tooth and Kenny decided he would fix it for her by putting epoxy on it LOL. Jennifer said when she read the ingredients for the epoxy she thought Kenny might be trying to kill her hahaha, but it was truly just Kenny's way to fix everything. Kenny showed me that he loved to pop wheelies on his motorcycle to mess with Jennifer when she was on his bike. Jennifer said, I can't tell you how many times I almost peed my pants when he would tell me to hold on and pull a wheelie. Kenny showed me that Jennifer had a condo or apartment near the shop that he lived and worked at and he said that they would spend time there together. Jennifer said yes, he would come to my condo that was just down the street from his shop and spend time with me. This was Kenny's way of stepping forward and sending his love to Jennifer as well as let her know that he is watching over her from Heaven. I have to say, this was one of the coolest connections I've made in some time because it allowed me to take a step back and connect a close friend with someone.

Jennifer also had another motorcycle rider coming through in her reading. This man who was coming through is Jennifer's uncle in life. He told me that he passed in a motorcycle accident with no helmet on. He showed me that he was hit by a truck and he said the truck hit me. He wanted Jennifer to know that he did not cross the line and the semi driver was dozing off on the road. Jennifer said well, that changes everything because we were told that my uncle was the one who hit the truck and it was kind of a relief to know that the truck had hit him because they truly just couldn't understand how their uncle had hit that truck.

There were so many more validation than I could even begin to place in this story. But the biggest validation of all was that a Father's Love for his little girl transcends life and passing for it is eternal.

I gave away a reading on my page in a random drawing for people who were willing to share the link to my book on their page. A woman named Jeska who has been on my page for some time was the winner of that reading. What was amazing about Jeska being drawn at this time was that she was originally drawn to my page because her Fiancé had passed to Heaven. I had even reached out to Jeska some time back and sent her a few messages in IM without her even asking for these messages from her Fiancé to let her know he was in Heaven and watching over she and her daughter. But, there was a new feeling when Jeska and I got on the phone to make arrangements for a time and day for her call with me. I had a young male coming through for Jeska, but it wasn't her Fiancé...... We set a time and day for her reading and it was just 2 days ago. When Jeska called me, she had asked if her boyfriend could join her on the call and I told her I didn't mind that at all.

Jeska and her boyfriend called me for the reading and I told Jeska that I wanted to talk to her about her Brother in Heaven. Jeska's Brother Eric had recently passed. I told Jeska that when I ask her brother about his passing, he tells me that it is Drug related. Jessica said, yes it was. Eric went on to tell me that he had fought an addiction in life for some time. He said that his addiction was with Heroin and that he absolutely did not take his life on purpose, but that his actions of using the drug had brought about his passing. Jeska said, yes, my brother fought an addiction with Heroin in life and he did not take his life intentionally, but we believe he did pass from the drug. Eric went on to show me that a Male that he lived with at the time of his passing found him and tried all he could to help him. He said there was nothing more that could have been done to save him. Jeska said, yes, our Uncle found him and I will tell him that he said this and hopefully it will bring him some comfort. Her brother showed me that he was living with 5 people in a family member's home at the time of his passing and he wanted to Thank this family member for always keeping his door open to him in life to come back when he needed. Jeska said, yes, that is our Grandfather's home and there were 5 living there. He went on to tell me, "I got Bad Drugs."

Jeska and her boyfriend gasped as I said these words because they had wondered if this had been the case, but weren't sure. Eric had answered their question before they even had to ask me. I assured Jeska that he was still taking responsibility, for no matter what was wrong with the drugs, he was the one that decided to use them and he was taking responsibility for his actions in that. Jeska understood her brother's words.

Eric then told me that he used to love to smoke marijuana in life as well. He said, my sister has my pipe now and Jeska laughed as she said yes, I have it saved.

Eric wanted to send his love to Jeska's boyfriend who was listening in on the call as well. He made me feel as though they were close in life and he told me that her boyfriend is going to be getting a tattoo in honor of him. Jeska's boyfriend simply said wow, I am getting a tattoo and he was amazed that Eric knew this. Eric spoke of his friend's souped up truck and he made me feel as though they had gone mudding with one another back in the day. Jeska's boyfriend said he does have a souped up truck and he and Eric had done some offroading back in the day together. Eric then told me that his sister is planning to get two tattoos in honor of him and it's going to be badass he said. She said yes, I am getting two tattoos for my brother. She said one is in addition to a tattoo that I already have and another is a tattoo of his very own. Eric wanted to send his love to his father is well and you made me feel as though dad is taking his passing really hard.

Eric took me to the time after his passing and he made me feel as though some of the family may have had an issue with him being cremated but he wanted his family to know that it's okay. Eric said, why spend the money on Burying my ass, I'm good lol! He was trying to make light of a situation that had been difficult for his family and Jeska understood the situation very well. She had tried her best to honor her brother in the best way that she knew how and so he was cremated. Eric showed me that Jeska has plans to share his ashes with numerous members in the family and he was very grateful that she is doing this. Jeska said yes, we have not gotten his ashes back yet but I do plan to share them with numerous people in the family so that they may honor him in their very own way. I told her I was very proud of her and the family for making this beautiful gesture of love because it truly doesn't matter to them in heaven what happens to their body after they passed. What matters most is that their family find comfort in how they honor Eric themselves. Eric told me that his sister had dressed him really cool for his memorial prior to being cremated. She said yes, I put him in his jersey that he loves. Jeska said, can he tell me something about what was placed with him in his casket? I said, well, when you asked me that he is showing me a cigarette? She laughed and laughed and said no, it wasn't a cigarette, it was a joint hahaha it was such a cool validation because he would be immediately answering a question she had asked! Jeska said that a close friend of Eric's had written on a joint and placed it with her brother. She later sent me pictures of it and we have included them in the story. What a cool gesture to honor her friend.

Eric told me that his friends and family had a big party in honor of him after his passing. Jeska said yes, we absolutely did! Eric said, they were lining up shots for me! Jeska said yes we did! She sent me a picture of the shots lined up in a row they had done for her brother to honor him.

Eric was showing me a baby in his hands that he made me feel his sister had lost this baby early on in pregnancy. I asked her if she had lost a baby and she began to cry and she said yes. I said, please know that your brother has your baby boy safe in His Hands In Heaven. Jeska didn't previously know of the sex of the baby and she had lost because it was so early in her pregnancy but it was a comfort to know now that she has a baby boy in heaven with her brother. I had to laugh when Eric's spunky personality came out as he told me to tell her, "It's okay, I already named him after myself ha ha". We all got a good laugh out of Eric's jokes from Heaven.

Eric told me that his baseball cap had been handed down to his girl-friend and he wanted to please send his love to her. He said that his sister also gave his girlfriend a shirt in honor of him and he wanted to thank his sister for doing that. He made me feel as though his girlfriend still has love letter saved from him. He said, my girlfriend tried to talk to me about getting some help and please tell her not to carry my burden and I love her so much. Jeska said she would be sure to pass along her brothers love.

Eric wanted to send his love to his mom as well and he told me that mom and dad were no longer together but he loves them both very much.

Eric made me feel like his hair was perfect in heaven. He said, you tried to make sure that my hair was perfect for my service and thank you. Jeska's boyfriend said that he actually spoke with the people at the funeral home to ensure that Eric's part was correct and his hair was the way he liked it because he was very particular about his hair in life.

The last validation that Eric gave me was that his sister is planning to cut all of her hair off! He jokingly said, oh shit, don't do it! Jeska laughed as she heard these words and then she told us that she had just thought a few days before of cutting her hair off completely but she hadn't told anybody. She said, I was only thinking of it. I thought this was one of the coolest validation that Eric gave us because it lets his sister know that he hears even her thoughts. It was a private thought she hadn't shared with anyone but Eric knew.

Eric will continue to watch over his family throughout their lives as he guides them on their paths. He will hear them always and there isn't a milestone in life that will happen without him there at their side. I was blessed to have been able to give this gift to Jeska so soon after her brother's passing. It was an honor to meet her feisty brother Eric ♡

Last night I did a Skype reading for Keri. She had her husband and Mom join her for the reading. I had previously done a reading for Keri sometime back. During that reading, I connected her with her beautiful son Blake in heaven who has passed in a vehicle accident at the age of 16. People often ask if they can do more than one reading and I always say yes because Spirit truly gives me new validations for each and every reading.

As Blake stepped forward in last night's reading, one of the first validation that he wanted to give was for his dad he was sitting with Mom on the screen. Blake said that Dad had helped him to pick out his car and he wanted to thank dad for this. He told me that he really wanted a sports car like any sixteen-year-old would I'm sure and then he laughed and said I didn't get my sports car and dad said yes, he told me that he wanted a sports car and no he didn't get a sports car haha. You see, the man in front of me on the screen was Blake's step dad in life but Blake still referred to him as his dad. There are no partial titles in heaven smile emoticon.

I looked over at Blake's Grandma and I said to her, Blake tells me that you started a prayer chain for him at your church after he passed to heaven and he wanted to thank you for this and let you know that he received all of the beautiful prayers that were sent his way. You see, Grandma truly wasn't a believer in mediums, but Blake wanted to assure her that this truly was him and what better way to let her know that then to set her mind at ease that he truly did receive her prayers with God in Heaven. Grandma seemed a bit taken back when I brought up this validation and she looked at me on the screen and she said yes, I did start a prayer chain for him at my church. It was a beautiful way for Blake to start this reading.

Blake told me that his family had 2 services for him when he passed to heaven and he wanted his family to know that he attended both services. Kari said, yes, we did two services for him because there was a delay in his burial service. Blake wanted his mom to know that he was aware of this delay and supported her through this difficult journey of waiting to bury her son.

Blake told me that his little sister is going to start a new school soon. Mom said yes, our youngest daughter was just registered for kindergarten. Blake said, she's already reading mom and she's doing great! Mom laughed a little and said wow yes she is reading already.

At this point in the reading I had to laugh because Blake said holy crap, my grandma just realized that this is all real! Haha

Blake told me that the memorial on the side of the road in honor of him had recently been redone and he loves it very much. His family said that yes, his memorial had just been redone. Blake then showed me that his family had balloons out in honor of him today. Blake showed me that one of the balloon went up out of their hands and into a tree and he was laughing as he tild me that he made this happen. Keri said yes, we were out at his memorial today because it is his birthday and we had brought balloons with us in honor of him. She went on to say that one of the balloons slipped out of her hands and went up into the air and into a nearby tree. Grandma was in awe that I knew this because she was there to witness this site as well. It was Blake's way of saying that they were not alone in honoring him today. Blake was then laughing and told me that someone was talking about climbing up the tree to get the balloon out. Keri laughed at this because Blake's little sister had in fact talked about climbing the tree herself to get the balloon down but of course they didn't get it because it was too high. Blake told me that his family is getting cake for him tonight and he wanted them to know that he will be with them. The family said yes, we are actually planning to go to The Cheesecake Factory for dinner in honor of his Birthday after this reading is over. Wow! Very cool! Blake also told me that Mom was doing something with a candle for him today and Mom said yes, I was actually in a store looking at an orange candle that I thought of buying in honor of Blake. Even in those Quiet Moments where no one else is around, it was Blake's way of letting mom know that she wasn't alone.

Blake showed me that Mom is talking to the kids at his school in honor of him and he wanted to thank her for this. Blake went on to tell me that his choir saying for him and he wanted the choir to know how much he loved this beautiful gesture. Mom said yes, his choir did sing at his funeral services for him. Blake said, my choir just won a championship and I was there with them every moment of the way cheering them on from heaven. Mom said that she was going to let his friends know this because they would love to hear that Blake was at their side and they did in fact just win a championship in choir.

Blake said that his parents still have a space for him in their home and he loved this. He told me that his family was going to pass his video games down to someone who needed them and he thanked them for the gesture of this. Mom said yes, he still has a room in our home and we did in fact plan to donate his video games to a child that was less fortunate but someone beat us to it and already donated one to him so we still have Blake's game.

Blake told me that Dad wants a new truck and dad started laughing. Dad said yeah Blake, tell your mom haha. I said to Dad, I think he just did haha. I said, Blake tells me you want a big Ford truck and dad said yes, that's actually one that I have been looking at getting. I turned to Mom and said Mom, Blake says we could go mudding in this truck LOL and everyone got a really good laugh out of Blake trying to help Dad get a truck from heaven.

Blake wanted me to talk to all of his family about the guilt they are carrying associated with his passing. He wanted me to tell them to please put the guilt down that they are carrying. He said, I was old enough to drive. It truly wasn't your fault. He wanted them to put away the what if and the could have and should have and truly just focus on the legacy of love that he left behind for them in life. He told me that he blessed them with more strength than they ever knew they could carry when he passed to heaven. Blake also said, Dad I know we butted heads from time to time but please know how much I love you.

Blake then told me that his biological dad got a tattoo in honor of him and he wanted to send his love and thanks to his biological father for getting this tattoo as well. He told me that he has more sisters at his dad's house that he would also like to send his love to. Blake told me that one of his sisters had recently moved out of Dad's house and he was watching over her as well. Blake knew that there was a separation between his sisters and mom right now and he didn't want to be the reason for that separation. He knew how very hard his passing was on his mom and made me feel as though she just needed to do the best that she could to find her happiness and hopefully his family will come back around and support and love her but for now he wanted mom to know that he is at her side. Mom understood this very well and we continued on.

Blake made me feel as though mom was planning to put his shoes out on display. Mom said yes, I had actually given his shoes to Blake's girlfriend after he passed to heaven and I recently asked her if she would mind giving them back so that I could place them in a shadow box with his clothing that he last wore and put it on display.

Blake told me that his mom has a tattoo in honor of him as well and he showed me that her husband was at her side when she got it. Mom actually stood up on her chair in front of a Skype screen so that she could place her foot in front of the camera while balancing on her husband to show me her beautiful tattoo that was written in Blake's handwriting. His handwriting turned into a tattoo read "Mom, I love you a million pounds, Blake"

Blake told me that his family made a trip in honor of him after his passing and he wanted to let them know that he was with them for this trip to the beach that they took. Mom said wow, you're good. She said that when the holidays came and Blake was not there to celebrate them, they decided to take a trip to the beach instead of staying home and feeling as though they were celebrating holidays without him. It was beautiful for him to let him know that he didn't miss that trip.

Blake told me that they will be calling his name at graduation this year. Mom said yes, one of his friends called and asked me if she could speak about Blake in Her speech at graduation. Blake said that he wouldn't be missing this from heaven and he would be at his grandma's side as she attended his graduation in honor of him.

Blake made me feel as though mom and dad are talking about getting married again or going back to where they were married. Mom and dad said yes, we are actually talking about taking a trip back to where we were married. I said well, he'll be on that trip too.

Blake did an amazing job in sharing his love for his family. He gave his grandma faith that she didn't know was missing and love to a stepfather who truly needed to know that Blake respected him as a dad in his life as well. I watched as Blake gave his Mom healing in her soul that she needed so much. I left that reading with a big smile on my face and said, way to go Blake.

Last week, I did a phone reading giveaway for the people on my page who have supported my journey with my new book. In that give away, a woman named Pam was announced as the winner. Pam didn't expect to win when she entered because she was halfway around the world in Australia. But Heaven didn't care about her distance from me as She was drawn. At first, Pam was not sure that she would be able to take the gift that I was giving her because we weren't sure how we would connect with one another. A phone option just didn't seem to be something she could do and so I offered that we could do her reading via Skype to save her the cost of long-distance charges. Last night, Pam and I were on a Skype conversation around the world from one another that was intensely beautiful. Here is her story because she has allowed me to share it with each of you.

As I began Pam's reading, I instantly felt as though I had her son coming through from heaven. When I asked her son to please tell me about his passing, he told me that his passing was sudden and unexpected. I asked him to start showing me more about his passing and he made me feel as though he had issues within his brain associated with his passing. Her son Trav told me that his issues within his brain where previous to his passing as well. He then made me feel as though I was clenching my teeth as if I was having a seizure. I asked Pam if her son had issues with seizures in life for some time and Pam said yes, he had epilepsy. He then told me that his seizure happened in a remote place with no one else around. He showed me that he was on the water when his seizure occurred. He told me, I was in the boat one moment and in the water the next moment. He wanted his mom to know that he left his body in spirit before his body struggled with in the water. Mom said yes, he was on a kayak trip alone when he suffered a seizure out on the water and ended up in the water because of his seizure. Trav later corrected me and told me that he wasn't completely alone because he showed me that he had his dog with him on the kayak when he had the seizure. Pam said yes, he did have his dog with him in his kayak when he passed who did survive the swim. Trav told me that he usually he would go with groups when he kayaked but not this time. He made me feel as though it took them over a day to find him after he passed but he wanted his mom to know that he was peaceful during that time. These words were comforting for his Pam as I know they would be for any Mom.

Trav began to show me that he lived his life completely to its fullest regardless of his epilepsy. He made me feel as though he truly wasn't going to let a seizure stop him from his dreams. He showed me himself riding motorcycles and climbing mountains and skydiving as well as many other things. Pam said yes, my son climbed Mount Everest and he skydived and he rode motorcycles and so much more. Trav then told me that his brother has inherited his motorcycle since his passing and he loves that his brother has his motorcycle. Pam said yes, his brother does have Trav's motorcycle. Trav said that his brother was given some private time with him after his passing and he wanted his brother to know that he was with him during that very difficult time. Pam said yes, his brother had to identify Trav's body. Trav said that his brother tried to keep mom from seeing his body when he passed and he was very grateful that his brother did this to protect mom. Pam said yes, my son suggested I not see him once they recovered him so that I can remember him for how he lived and not for the way that he passed. I thought it was beautiful of her son to protect his mom in that way.

Trav told me that his mom and brother are getting tattoos in honor of him and he was pretty excited about this from Heaven. Pam was excited to hear that Trav knew of their plans because they just booked flights with the airlines to go get these tattoos that Trav spoke of!

Trav showed me that he has his father with him in heaven and he wanted to set Mum's my mind at ease that he and his father had indeed reunited in heaven.

Trav told me that Mom is getting a wind chime in honor of him. Pam said yes, I have been looking for a wind chime in honor of my son but I just haven't decided on one yet. Trav told me that his friends honored him with stickers with his name on it and he wanted to send his love to each and every one of them. Mom said yes, his friends did have stickers printed for him that they handed out to one another.

Trav then took me to his memorial and made me feel as though his friends dressed really cool in honor of him and he was very thankful for this. Mom said yes, his friends dressed in Bermuda shorts at his memorial in honor of him. Trav then said that his mom dressed him really cool for his funeral as well and he wanted to thank her for honoring him in that way. He said, it wasn't your average suit! Mom said yes, I put him in his suit jacket with Bermuda shorts and flip-flops on in his casket. It was a beautiful way for this mother to honor her son and the way that he always lived.

I asked Pam if she had any questions to ask her son and she simply asked, can he tell me about the watch? I was glad that she didn't give me more information than that but I didn't understand what he was showing me. Trav showed me a watch stopping and of course it didn't mean anything to me but I thought I would ask Pam why it was that Trav was showing me a watch stopping? Pam said that since Trav's passing, his brother wears Trav's watch in honor of him, but the watch stopped just one time for 4 hours and then started again and it's never had trouble since and they had wondered if that was from Trav. What a cool validation of a great big yes that was me!

Pam's husband came through during the reading as well to send his love. He made me feel as though he had cancer at the end if his life. He made me feel as though he found his cancer quite late in its stages but he wanted his wife to know that he was okay. He said, please tell my wife that I was here to meet our son. Her husband showed me that he loved to fish in life and made me feel as though he is fishing with his son in Heaven. Pam said yes, my husband did passed from cancer and he was an avid fisherman in life. Her husband wanted to thank her in a big way for allowing him to pass at home where he was comfortable. He said that she still lived in the home now that he passed it. Pam said yes, I still live in our home.

Her husband showed me that she and her son who is still living worked on vehicles with one another in life and he wanted to please send his love to their son. He told me that he and his son in Heaven share a name and she said yes, they do share a name. Pam's husband told me that Pam does her a wind chime in honor of him and Pam said, yes, I do.

Both Pam's husband and son came together in her reading to bring her healing that she never thought she would receive. The smile on her face on my Skype screen really said it all when she told me thank you because I could feel it through her smile that she had found healing. It surely was a beautiful day for both Pam and I even though we were a world and even a day apart since I was in Arizona and she was in Australia. And, I have to say that Trav is one cool dude.

When I gave away the 1st of the month phone reading, I had someone in Heaven who made me feel like I also needed to Gift some time to another person besides the winner. When I posted on Misty's entry, I told her that she hadn't won, but that I personally wanted to give her some time in a reading on the phone. You see, I actually needed to get to her Husband because their son in Heaven was saying we needed to help his Dad. When Misty and I got on the phone with one another to work out a time and day to speak, you could imagine the smile in my soul when Misty asked if her Husband could join us on the call... Um, YES!!!!! (Thanks for working that one out Kid)

Misty and her husband and daughter called me last night for their reading. Misty has been on my page for some time, but we have never spoken of who she has in Heaven. I could hardly get through my opening speech when I felt as though her Son was making me trip on my words because he was so eager to speak with his family and so, I said, well, I guess we are starting ha ha.

I told Misty and her husband that I had a young male who made me feel like their son coming through. Misty said that she and her husband do have a son in Heaven named Taylor. I began to ask Taylor to take me through his passing. Taylor said that his passing was sudden and unexpected. He made me feel as though he had taken an impact in a vehicle accident. Misty said, yes, he passed in a vehicle crash. As Taylor gave me more information about his passing, he told me that he took the car too fast and that he was taking responsibility for his actions in driving fast that day. Misty said, yes, speed was a factor in the crash. Taylor showed me that he was only partially ejected from the vehicle as it rolled because he made me feel as though he was kind of restrained. Misty said, yes, that is exactly correct, he was partially ejected from the vehicle just as you said because he was kind of restrained. I knew there were about to be cuss words flying out of my mouth, but it was the essence of her son and when it comes to making sure that a family feels their loved one, I don't use a filter.... Taylor showed me that he saw the crash coming and he said, "Oh Shit, we're Fucked" and left his body to watch from a place of spirit because he was trying to get the top of his seat belt over himself and he said, "I didn't fucking get it on in time, so I left my body". Misty confirmed that her son didn't have the bottom belt over his lap, but had the top part of the seat belt partially restraining him just as he had described. She giggled as the cuss words came out of my mouth and said, "That's my Son". Taylor showed me that his body lived for a small amount of time after the accident. He said that the room was full of loved ones when he passed, but showed me that 5 extremely important people stood around his bed when he went to Heaven. Misty said, yes, the room was full and there were 5 close family members at his bedside. He wanted them to know he hadn't suffered and was in the room with them in Spirit. Taylor laughed as he said, "They were climbing in bed with me!!" Misty said, in that emotional moment that they had ended up on the bed with Taylor. Taylor told me to tell his Mom and Dad that his "Brother" is at his side in Heaven. I then saw a young male who looked to be the same age as Taylor at his side in Heaven. Misty said that Taylor's friend "Brother" was in the passenger seat of Taylor's car and he passed in the accident with Taylor that day. It was beautiful that the boys were together. I didn't focus on Taylor's friend Jody only because we didn't have his family with us during the reading, but he was vibrant, beautiful, and Spunky ha ha and we carried on....

Taylor took his ball cap off of his head and handed it to his Dad. I said, Taylor tells me Dad has his ball cap. Dad didn't respond, but Misty said, yes, he does and that is very significant. Taylor then told me that his family wears something in honor of him on their wrists? Misty said, yes we all have bracelets in honor of Taylor. Taylor took me to Mom's back and told me that Mom wears a tattoo in honor of him on her back. Misty said, yes, I sure do. Taylor told me that his sister was wearing shirts for him. Misty said that Taylor's sister had a shirt on that was made in honor of her brother as we spoke. I said, he tells me his sister wrote a story about him? Misty asked her daughter if she had written a story of her brother and she said she had. When Misty answered me that her daughter had written a story about their son, she said, None of us knew she wrote that. It was Taylor's way of letting his family know that he still sees them since his passing.

Taylor took me outside and told me that trees were planted in honor of him after he passed. Misty said, yes, they planted a few trees for him. I said, he says that there is a plaque in honor of him out near the trees. Misty said, yes, we put a Sign in honor of the boys on the side of the road where the accident happened with a reminder for others to watch their speed. I told Misty that I was proud of her for taking this and turning it into a way to honor the boys and help others at the same time.

Taylor then took my attention back to Dad. Taylor put me in a Jeep and made me feel like he and Dad did some off roading in the Jeep together. I think Dad was a bit taken back by all of this and Misty continued to answer for the group, but I knew that his son was reaching him with love because of the silence from Dad. Misty said, My husband Used to have a Jeep and he and our Son did some offroading together in that Jeep for sure. Taylor told me that his Dad was really angry when he passed in the accident and he wanted Dad to know that it was really okay for him to be angry. Taylor understood that his own mistake in driving that day caused his Dad's pain and anger because of that pain. He wanted Dad to know that he didn't need to feel guilty for feeling angry when he passed because he was taking responsibility for driving too fast that day. He knew that Dad's anger came from Love. Misty said they understood this very well. Taylor then told me that he and Dad had built/worked on his car together and he loved his car. Taylor said, "I was into Badass Cars". Misty laughed and said, yes my Husband and Taylor had worked on and built Taylor's car together.

Taylor told me that a Male his parents age just had a tire blow out and he wanted to send his love to him as well. Misty said that yes, his Uncle just had a tire blow out! Taylor told me that his Grandma lights candles for him and he wanted to Thank her for this and tell her how much he loves her. He started playing the song "I Believe" for me at this moment and Misty said "I Believe" is very significant for Mom because many of the things that she has in honor of Taylor say "I Believe" on them! Wow Taylor!! Way to Go Buddy!!!

Taylor handed me a curl of his hair and told me that Mom has his Curl saved. Misty said, yes, I have a curl of his hair saved. I said, he shows me himself with curly hair. Misty said, that is good to hear because they had shaved my son's hair off when he was in the accident. I said, well, he has it back now that he is in Heaven for sure!

Taylor told me he had Misty's Dad with him in Heaven as well. Dad came through briefly to send his love. He told me he passed from Cancer. Dad said he was in the Military in life and he wanted to send his love to his family, but he quickly stepped back because he knew that the healing they needed today was from Taylor.

Taylor told me at the end of the reading, "My Dad needed this more than my Mom". Taylor Thanked me for helping to Save his Dad with him from Heaven. He needed his Dad to know that he is okay and he is still with him. He did a beautiful job in making sure Dad left that conversation with no doubt that his Feisty Son is still perfect as he ever was from Heaven. Misty Thanked me for giving them my time for this reading. I honestly couldn't imagine not giving it to them, because Heaven asked me to and I always listen to these requests.... My night was blessed with Love by this reading. Thank you Taylor!

Kaisa has previously had a reading with me and she also attended one of my group readings. Kaisa contacted me last week to schedule a phone reading at my earliest convienience. I was booked for the week when she contacted me and the next available appointment I had would be for today, August 15th, 2016. I told Kaisa of this opening and she said it would work well for her and so we scheduled it. Little did I know that Heaven was behind that scheduling!

As Kaisa and I got on the phone with one another today, there were things that I knew in advance of this reading because she had previous readings with me. In those previous readings, her beautiful baby boy, Gunnar, who was "born still" at 37 weeks of her pregnancy came through for his Mommy. Today, Gunnar began to come through immediately with a validation that took my breath away!! Gunnar said, My Mommy and Daddy are Celebrating me today! Kaisa said, Yes, we are, today is Gunnar's Birthday! Kaisa hadn't asked to schedule her reading on this day.... She asked for my earliest opening.... Gunnar made sure in advance that his Mommy would be sharing his birthday with Heaven. I had beautiful goose bumps when he said this! Gunnar went on to show me that his Mommy has a cake for him on his birthday and he loves it. Kaisa said, yes, we are having a cake for his birthday today. Gunnar said, Mommy and Daddy are having a balloon release for me today too. Kaisa said, yes, we are. Gunnar then showed me that Mommy is having a Birthday Dinner for him and he wanted his Mommy to know that he isn't missing out on his dinner. He showed me that Mommy invited someone to his dinner as well. Kaisa said, yes I have been cooking since yesterday for this dinner in honor of Gunnar and, I invited a girlfriend to join us and she will be here for the dinner as well. Gunnar then showed me a reference to chocolate candy? I said, are you having chocolate candy for his birthday too because he is showing me chocolate candy for his birthday? Kaisa said, I have a Very Special Grandpa who sends a chocolate bar for each Grandkid on their birthday as a tradition. I told her to please send his love to his Great Grandpa from Heaven.

Gunnar then told me that his Mommy and Daddy are talking about getting a new Puppy at home. Kaisa said, oh wow, yes, my husband and I are talking about getting a new lab puppy because a friend's dog just had a litter. I said, he is giving me a hunting dog reference with this? Kaisa was in awe at this validation because just TODAY, she had a conversation in which her Hubby really wants one of these puppys and is trying to talk her into one, told her that The SIRE of the litter is actually a Hunting Champion Blood Line. WOW Gunnar!!! Way to let your Mommy and Daddy know that you are watching over them!

Gunnar told me that he has a sister and he wants to send his love to her. He said that his sister is drawing pictures for him and he loves them. Kaisa said, yes, he has a sister and she draws a heart with wings in honor of her brother all the time. She said that her daughter actually writes her own name and then puts the heart with wings next to it in honor of her brother as well. I said, he tells me one of his sister's drawings in honor of him is on your Fridge? Kaisa said, yes, there is a picture she drew for our baby on the fridge in honor of him. Gunnar showed me that his sister is in Kindergarten and as I asked Kaisa about this, she said yes, she is. Gunnar then showed me his sister wanted to get on the bus to school but couldn't because Mommy didn't let her and he giggled about this. Kaisa said, yes, our little girl had her first day of Kindergarten recently and she really wanted to ride the bus on her first day, but Mommy wanted to take her to her very first day of school and so Kaisa didn't let her ride the bus the first day and Gunnar's sister wasn't happy at all about missing her first day of school bus ride hahaha.... Kaisa said, no worries, she has ridden the bus ever since and she got ice cream after her first day of school for the forced ride with Mommy haha. Gunnar also told me that his sister wanted a different backpack than the one she got lol. Kaisa said, wow, yes, she really wanted a Spider-Man backpack and Kaisa and her husband really wanted her to have a more sturdy backpack and so they got her a Jan Sport backpack instead, but they got her a little Spider-Man Keychain to hang on her backpack instead. It was apparent that little Gunnar was watching over his sister from Heaven all they way down to her school supplies ha ha. Gunnar also showed me a little girl with glasses with his sister. Kaisa said, yes, our daughter just made a new friend down the street from us that wears glasses..... AWESOME!

Gunnar told me that his Mommy just got a new necklace in honor of him. Kaisa said that she had actually recently ordered a new necklace in honor of her son, so recently in fact, that it hasn't yet arrived at her home! I said, did you just curb check your car Kaisa? She said, I backed over a curb today.... Aww Gunnar, way to watch out for your Mama.

Gunnar then gave me a special validation for his Mommy and Daddy.... He said, Mommy and Daddy are having a new baby now. Kaisa said, yes, I am 9 weeks pregnant right now. I said, Gunnar wants you to know that it is going to be okay Mama..... I could hear the relief in her voice as she said she had worried about that from the moment she found out she is pregnant. Gunnar told me that Mommy is planning to name the new baby after him and he loves the idea. Kaisa said, yes, we are planning to incorporate his name in the baby's name.

Gunnar told me that his Daddy just got a new and better job and he wanted Daddy to know that he helped him to get the job. Kaisa said, yes, my husband did just get a new and better job recently and he will love to hear that Gunnar helped him to get the job.

Gunnar told me that he has an Aunt that lives in another state and he said she was just talking about wanting to come see his Mommy. He wanted to send his love to his Aunt. Kaisa said, yes, I have a sister who lives out of state and just this morning, we were texting back and forth about how each of us wishes we were closer so we could be with each other today.

Gunnar also told me that there is another Sister like person in his Mommy's life that wants a little girl. Kaisa said, oh yes, I have a cousin who is also like a sister to me and she always talks about wanting a little girl when she has her first baby in life.....

Gunnar did a beautiful job of making his Birthday Special for his Mommy, Daddy, and Sister.... He will be with them every moment as they celebrate him on his special day.

People often ask me if babies can communicate with me just someone who was older when they passed would? I say, Yes!!! Babies have eternal souls just as we do. They are limitless when it comes to communicating with me and watching over you. This little boy didn't have any life experience with Kaisa and her family outside of the beautiful time he spent in her womb. But, that hasn't stopped him from sharing their life experiences with them now and for always from Heaven.

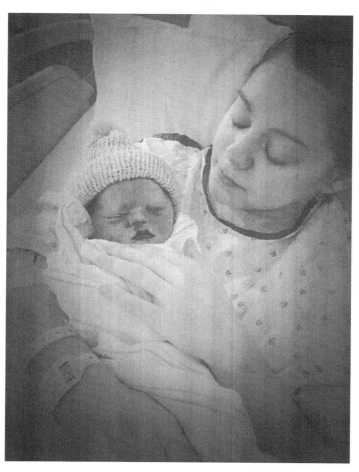

I had a reading yesterday with a woman named Ladeena. I knew in advance that she intended to include her daughters on the line for the phone reading as well. What I didn't know was that when Ladeena called with one daughter on the line and we were bridging her second daughter onto the call, that the daughter we were adding had NO idea that we were calling her for a reading with a Medium. Yep, Surprise for both of us lol. Mom (Ladeena) said, this is my daughter Kari and she has no idea who you are. I started to introduce myself and Kari said, "Are you a Medium?!" I introduced myself and began to tell her a little bit about myself when spirit interrupted me and I said, well, let's just get started because I have a young girl in Heaven who makes me feel like MOM is here because she says Mom, Mom, Mom! Kari understood and missed the sound of those words from her little girl in Heaven as she cried and said, yes, that is my daughter, Kadyn. I said, oh boy, I hope you have a Kleenex with you right now.... She said, I am looking for napkins, and anything I can find and if I have to, I will use my shirt sleeve.

Typically, one of the first things I ask of a loved one in Heaven is for them to tell me about their passing. Kadyn told me that her passing was sudden and unexpected. She told me that she had taken an impact to her head and chest in a vehicle accident. But, she then told me, I wasn't in the vehicle. Kadyn then showed me that she was hit by a truck and my heart sank at what she showed me next....... She said, He saw me when he hit me but he didn't stop..... She told me that the man who hit her was intoxicated at the time that he hit her as well. Kari cried as her little girl began to give me the beginning details of her daughter's passing as she validated back that the words I spoke to her were true. A man had hit her little girl and never stopped to help her. He did have marijuana in his system when he was tested as well. Kadyn later showed me that she was getting on the bus for school and the bus had all of the stop lights on when she was trying to board. She wanted me to tell her Mommy to stop feeling guilty for not being there at the bus stop because no one could have changed what happened to her that day. Kadyn showed me that another Mom tried desperately to help her and she wanted to thank her for all she did to get help, but she said, I left my body in spirit before that truck hit me because I knew it was my time to go to Heaven. Kadyn showed me that she watched the truck hit from a beautiful and protected place in spirit to let her Mommy know she did not suffer. Kadyn went on to show me that another female tried helping her as well. Grandma Ladeena spoke for Kari who was in tears to tell me that yes, the bus driver was a female and also tried to help.

Kadyn told me that one of the ladies on the phone was planning a trip to come and see her at the time of her passing. Kadyn's Aunt on the phone said, yes, I had a trip planned to come and visit her. Kadyn then told me that she has brothers and she wants to send her love to them. Kari said, yes, I have sons now as well. I said, she shows me that she handed you babies from Heaven and she is telling me that one of her baby brothers was sick when he was a tiny baby and she wants you to know she made sure he wouldn't be sick as she watched over him from Heaven. Kari cried as she realized that the complications she had with her baby boy were watched over by her little girl in Heaven.

Kadyn showed me that her Mommy has done balloon releases in her honor and she loves that Mommy writes notes to her on the balloons. Kari said, yes, we have done numerous balloon releases in her honor. Kadyn said, I have 2

Daddies and I want to send my love to them both. Kari said, yes she has a biological Father and then she has my husband she referred to as her Daddy as well.

Kadyn took me back to the details of her passing when she told me that the man who hit her was arrested. She said, He didn't get as much time as my Mommy wanted, but, he did answer for my passing and she wanted her Mommy to know it was okay that he didn't get more time because he would have to live with the knowledge that he saw her and didn't stop for the rest of his life which would be difficult. Kari said that he was convicted for Kadyn's passing and is serving time in Prison for her daughter's passing. She had hoped he would get more time than he thought. Kari cried as she said, he told the court he didn't see a child and didn't know he had hit a child.

Kadyn showed me her Mommy Marching up the steps of the court in her honor.

She made me feel as though Mommy had fought hard for her. She said, They tried to get the man let off of the charges given and her Mommy made sure this didn't happen. Kari said, yes, we marched up the stairs of the courts to get Kadyn's Law put into place to keep other children safe in the future.

Kadyn loved that her Mommy did this in her honor for others.

Kadyn then took me to her hair. She said, Mommy saved my Hair. I said, Did you save Kadyn's hair? Kari broke down in uncontrollable tears when I said this. She cried so hard she could hardly answer with the words, " I told Kadyn if this was her and this was real to bring up that I saved her hair" I said, she shows me that you have a curl saved of hers. Kari knew in this instant, that all of the words spoken before this validation were truly coming from her little girl. She knew in that moment that her little girl could still hear her. In that Moment, Kari knew that Heaven is for real... I could hear and feel the pain release from this Mommy who's little girl was filling her with love from Heaven.

Kadyn began to tell me about her brothers, like that one had just been recognized in school with a certificate. She told me that her little cousin was potty training and wearing big boy character undies. She told me that she shares a name in the family and Kari told me that one of Kadyn's brothers born after her passing has her name as his middle name. Kadyn told me that Daddy is changing jobs and she is watching over this. She told me that she got the family's letters in Heaven and her Aunt on the phone said the family had written letters and placed them with her when she passed.

Kadyn told me that one of her brothers is going to play baseball, and Kari said, Oh wow, we just signed him up today. Kadyn told me one of her brothers loves to 4 wheel and Kari said, yes, she has a brother that loves to 4 wheel. Kadyn wanted to send her love to her Aunt who was not on the phone with us today who has a daughter as well. The ladies said they would be sure to send her love to her Aunt. Kadyn said, one of my brothers keeps falling down. Kari laughed a little when she told me that one of Kadyn's baby brothers is learning to walk and he falls down all the time...

Kadyn then took me to her school. She showed me that the school made a plaque in her honor. Kari said, yes, they did. She then showed me that the school also planted a tree in her honor and that this is where the plaque is. Kari again said, yes. I said, she tells me that you were there when they planted her tree. Kari said, yes, I was. I said, this seems weird, but I will say it, she makes me feel as though the school sings to her tree?

Kari cried as she said the school had planted the tree outside of the music room at Kadyn's school because Kadyn loved music! WOW!!! Go Kadyn!!!! Kadyn then said, Mommy has a video of her singing. Grandma Ladeena said, Yes, we do. Kari cried as she recalled Kadyn had to miss her school performance when they had a trip planned to visit Grandma Ladeena. So, since they knew how much Kadyn had worked on the program, they asked her to perform the program for them and she did as they recorded every beautiful moment.

This was a surprise from beautiful Ladeena that her daughter Kari will never forget. There are no words for the healing that happens for a parent with a child in Heaven after being given the Peace that their child is more than okay, they are Perfect in Heaven's Arms. This was a day that I won't forget and I was Honored to be a part of such a beautiful surprise.

Some of you may remember that Bonnie won a phone reading last week here on my page. Today was Bonnie's day to connect with her loved ones in Heaven. It didn't take long to realize why I heaven had picked Bonnie for this reading.

As I began connecting with heaven for Bonnie, I had a young male stepping through for her. He told me, that's my mom. I ask Bonnie if she has a son in Heaven and she said yes, my son Mike. I began to ask Mike to tell me more about his passing. He told me that his passing was sudden and or unexpected. He made me feel as though I had taken an impact to my head. As I gave these validations to Bonnie, she said that yes they were correct. I began to pat my chest with one hand and this is my symbol that tells me that their loved one in heaven is taking responsibility for their passing. I told Bonnie of this gesture and said yes, my son did take his life. I asked Mike to take me through his passing and he did. Mike told me that he was home alone at the time that he passed. He showed me that his mom was at work. He said that he and his mom had spoken prior to his passing but he wanted her to know that it was okay because she was just truly being a mom in that moment. Mike went on to tell me that there was a relationship that had recently ended prior to his passing and the breakup had broken his heart. He made me feel as though he just truly didn't realize how loved he was in this world until he passed. He made me feel as though all of the little things that we go through from day-to-day just seemed so big in that moment that he chose to take his life. He showed me that he went into a secured place that his dad had a gun and he took his father's gun. He wanted to apologize to his father for using his gun and didn't want his dad to carry guilt because of that. He said Dad had it locked up just as it should have been. He made me feel as though after he took his life that his mom found him when he passed and he said, I never intended for you to see me that way Mom and for that I'm sorry. Mike told me that he hadn't left a note for his family on the day that he passed and he knows how much his mom wished he had. Bonnie cried as I said these words. She had found her son when he passed on that day. She had also sent him a text just prior to his passing and it was just one of those Mom texts and she said she wished she could have simply sent an I love you instead. I reminded her that her son wanted her to know that she was just truly being a mom in that moment and it's okay. Bonnie said she had searched and searched for a note from her son and she said that sometimes she still looks to make sure she didn't miss one but she has not found a note from him. I reminded her that he said he didn't leave a note and so this reading would now be the note that she's been missing out on.

Mike told me that he has a brother and he wants to send his love to his brother. He then jokingly said but, I'm the number one son. I asked Bonnie if he's her first son and she said yes he is my number one and first son. Mike then corrected me and told me that he actually has two other siblings and he told me there are three of us children. Bonnie said yes, I have 3 children. Mike told me that his brother got an F in school and he was giving him crap for it from heaven. Bonnie said yes, his brother failed one class and it affected his senior year. Mike told me that he has a sister as well and he said, my sister is getting married. Bonnie said yes, he does have a sister and she is getting married. I told Bonnie to please pass along to his sister that he would not be missing out on her special day from Heaven. Mike said, my sister is carrying me down the aisle and he showed me a vision in my mind of his sister's hand holding her bouquet. Bonnie said that her daughter doesn't know it yet but she purchased a bracelet that has a charm with her brother and grandmothers pictures on it that she was going to give to her daughter to wear on her wedding day down the aisle. This was Mike's way of telling his mom thank you for the beautiful gesture of love.

Mike wanted to talk about his dad. He made me feel as though his dad was taking his passing very hard and he wanted to surround His dad with love. Mike showed me an image of himself fishing with his dad and made me feel as though he loved fishing in life and he got that love from his dad. Bonnie said yes, he and his dad just loved to fish with one another and he did get his love for fishing from his dad. Mike told me that he and his dad spent much time Outdoors growing up. Mike told me that his dad has a tattoo in honor of him and he wanted his mom to tell his dad that he loves it! Bonnie said she would pass the information on to her husband although he is skeptic of Psychics. I told her that I completely understood him being skeptical because there are so many dishonest psychics out there, but at the same time I hoped that he would receive his son's love. Mike went on to tell me that his dad is actually planning a second tattoo in honor of him and he was very excited about this from heaven. Bonnie said, yes he is. Mike showed me that he loved to go mudding in his truck in life. He then told me that he and his dad wrenched on that truck together in life and he made me feel as though those were the some of the best time spent with his dad. Bonnie said, wow, yes they worked on that truck together and he did love Mudding. She said there is still mud on Mikes truck from his last outing. Mike told me that there was a memorial made in honor of him so that Mom would have a place to light candles for him and he said that Dad made this by hand. Bonnie said yes, my husband made a memorial area for me to light candles in honor of our son. Mike wanted his Dad to know just how much he loves him.

Mike told me that his mom is planning on getting a tattoo in honor of him as well. She said yes, I've been working on making a decision as to what kind of tattoo I wanted to get in honor of my son and she just made the decision on the tattoo she's getting. Mike said, my mom wears bracelets in honor of me and tell her thank you. Bonnie said, I wear a set of metal bracelets that my son gave me when he was a child in honor of him. Mike then put a button up shirt on me and made me feel as though it was his favorite and that his mom has this saved. Mom said yes, it's the same shirt he wore in his senior pictures and it's a button up shirt that I do absolutely have saved in honor of him.

Mike told me that someone was getting his boots tattooed on them in honor of him as well and he loves this! Bonnie was in awe of this validation because one of Mike's close friends is in fact getting a portrait of Mike's boots tattooed on her in honor of him.

Mike's biggest message of all today during our reading was, I love you. .... He had left behind a family that loves him with all of their heart and soul and he sees that now. He sees now how he could have done things differently and how very much his passing has affected those he loves. They are enough...

Before Rita called me last week, for her reading, I had a young male in Heaven telling me, "My Sister's coming!". You could imagine the giggle in my soul when Rita text me to say that her daughter had decided to join her for our reading at the last minute. I sent Rita a message back saying I didn't mind at all if her daughter joined us. Little did she know at that time that I already knew because of Heaven telling me, that Rita has a Son in Heaven and her daughter who would be joining us is his Sister.

When Rita and her daughter called me, I felt as though her son was coming through. It was cute how excited he was in Heaven to come through for his Mom and Sister, So much so, that I couldn't get through my short opening speech ha ha. I asked Rita's son Hayden, , to tell me about his passing and he began by telling me that he was sick at the end of his young life. Hayden made me feel as though his head was affected by his illness. Though he was sick for some time in life, he made me feel as though his passing became sudden and unexpectedly he said. Hayden told me that his family truly didn't have time in the end to realize they were facing his passing. Rita said, yes, my son was sick with a brain tumor. Rita went on to say that her son had surpassed the life expectancy predictions given by all of his doctors and his cancer had gone dormant for some time. They truly believed that he would get better, when suddenly the cancer was back leaving him with just months to live before his passing and just like her son said, they didn't have time that they thought they would because the cancer was so aggressive when it returned. He said that his Mom kept him home and took care of him through his illness and he wanted to Thank her for all that she had done for him. He then told me that he also has a 2nd Dad in the home with Rita and he said this Dad also helped to take care of him and he wanted to send his love to both his biological father as well as the Dad who lived with he and Rita at home because he had done so much for him. When her son told me that his passing was very recent, my heart ached for Rita when she responded that her son had only passed 2 months ago to Heaven. Hayden showed me that his Mom held him in her arms as he made his journey to Heaven. Hayden said that his sister who was joining us on this call was holding his hand.

He showed me that there were numerous people in the room when he passed and most were women, but he wanted to send his love to each of them for being there for him through his journey to Heaven. Rita said she would be sure to pass along her son's love.

Hayden told me that Rita and her Fiancé would be moving out of state soon. He said, please tell my Mom that she is not leaving me behind and I am going with her when she moves. Rita cried as I said these words because she is moving out of state and she said, there is no way you would have known that and she went on to say she has been feeling like she is leaving her son behind in the move because of the memories made in the home together. I said, he says his sister is not moving out of state and he wants her to know he will continue to watch over her here as well. I explained to the ladies that he could be in more than one place at a time since he is a perfect and limitless spirit now in Heaven. His sister said, yes, I am staying here and she was relieved to know her brother would be watching over her as well. I then asked him to give me more details about Mom's move, and he said, Mom is moving to an outdoorsy place and she is getting property in the move. As I asked Rita about this, she was floored because she and her Fiancé are in fact moving to an outdoorsy place where fishing will be at their doorstep and they are purchasing acreage in the move as well! I then asked him to give me a validation for his sister as well. He said, my sister is in a new relationship. She said, wow, yes, I am. I said, your brother tells me that you are moving in with this new guy? (I don't think Mom knew the news yet ha ha) His sister said that she had in fact been staying nights at her new boyfriend's home and they have spoken about moving in with one another recently and it is in the works. I said, your brother says he will not be missing out on your wedding day. As I said these words, his sister broke down in tears because when her little brother passed, and she found herself in this happy relationship, her fear was that her brother was going to miss her wedding day someday down the line in the future and it was breaking her heart. Her brother was going to ease those fears for her today from Heaven. He then showed me that his sister has a necklace hanging in honor of him on her rear view mirror of her car. She said, yes, I do have a necklace hanging there for him. I said, your brother tells me you are going back to school and he wants you to know how proud he is of you! His sister said, wow, yes, I am thinking of going back to school. I said, Hayden tells me you want to be a nurse so you can help other kids like him who have cancer. His sister had tears in her voice as she said her brother was right.

Hayden told me that someone in the family was talking about naming their son after him when it is born. Rita said, oh yes!!! There was a comment made by a family member that they wouldn't be able to have a baby in life with a woman who wouldn't let him name his first son after Hayden. I said, Oh WOW! I think Hayden loves the Ultimatum hahahaha

I told Rita that her son was showing me that she had saved some of his hair in honor of him. Again, Rita broke down in tears as she said, "There is absolutely no way that you would have known that I saved his hair!" Rita said that only she and her daughter had his hair saved and no one would have known they had saved it.

Hayden said, my family did a balloon release in honor of me and please tell them that I got their notes in Heaven that they wrote on the balloons. Rita said, yes, we did a huge balloon release in honor of him and it was beautiful to know that her son had seen the release they honored him with.

Hayden wanted his Mom to know he had found the larger dog with longer fur in Heaven when he arrived. Rita began to cry, because as her son was passing to Heaven, she had told her son that numerous loved ones would be there waiting for him and she also told him that he would find their lab Bo Bo when he arrived in Heaven who was the sweetest Lab (dog) they had in their family that had passed. I said, there must be a bandana story about Bo Bo because Bo Bo is sitting next to Hayden and Bo Bo is laughing about the bandana. Rita said, Wow, every time Bo Bo went to the groomers, they would put a bandana on him and she said that every time her Fiancé got Bo Bo home, they would have to immediately take the bandana off because it drove him nuts ha ha ha.

Hayden then said, Grandma is here with me too. Rita cried as I said these words because her beautiful loving Grandma was also one of the precious people in her life that she had told her son he would meet when he got to Heaven. Grandma made me feel as though she was sick at the end of her life. She said, I passed some time ago and I handed Hayden to Rita from Heaven when he was a baby. Grandma then wanted to Thank Rita for handing Hayden back to her in Heaven and she wanted Rita to know that he was safe in her keeping. Rita broke down at these words because you see, Grandma had passed before Hayden was born in life which was why she gave the reference to handing him to Rita as a baby.... Rita understood the validation of giving him back because she had asked her Grandmother out loud to please take care of her son as he arrived in Heaven. It was beautiful proof that Heaven hears us and that we are all together again when we get there.

I said, Hayden is showing me a skateboard and he says it is hanging up on the wall. Rita was again in awe because just earlier that morning, she had a conversation with her Fiancé about Hayden's skateboard that was hanging up on the wall in their garage. Her fiancé wanted to know what he should do with the skateboard and Rita asked him to leave it there for now until she makes a decision.... I had goose bumps on my arms as Rita said those words because this was beautiful Hayden's way of letting his Mom and Dad know that he was there for this conversation earlier that day. He is with them from Heaven and doesn't miss even the smallest details of their day like conversations about a skateboard on the wall.

Hayden told me that Mom was given houseplants in honor of him after his passing and he was laughing in Heaven when he said, "Mom is killing the plants!" hahahahahah... Rita began to laugh and laugh through her tears. I said, Hayden tells me you are watering them too much! Rita laughed some more at this validation because she does have house plants gifted in honor of her son and she said she has had no idea how to keep them alive and so she just keeps watering them because they are dying hahahahahahaha

Hayden did a beautiful job in bringing healing and love to his Mom and Sister. His legacy of love that he left behind for others in this world, shines through the love that I felt coming from his family as I connected them with Hayden. He may have only had a short time here on Earth with his family, but his strength, courage, and love will last for all eternity in the hearts of those that his life touched

You may remember that Angie won a reading here on my page. This last week she and I spent an hour on the phone with one another as I connected her with Heaven. As we began her reading, Angie's son Trevor began to come through from Heaven. I asked Trevor to please tell me of his passing and he told me that his passing was sudden and unexpected. He told me that he was on a motorcycle at the time of his passing. He showed me that he was hit by a large truck. Trevor said, My "Brother" is here with me in Heaven as well.

Trevor showed me that he and another young male were riding on the same bike with one another. Trevor showed me himself on the back of the bike with is buddy. Trevor jokingly said, "Normally we wouldn't be riding on the same bike together" He showed me the truck coming at the boys and he showed me that his friend who was driving the motorcycle tried with all of his might to lay the bike down, but there just wasn't time. Trevor showed me that the man driving the truck had fallen asleep at the wheel just before he hit the boys. Angie said, Yes, my son was on a motorcycle when he was hit by a truck driver. She said that both her son Trevor and one of his best friends passed in this accident. The boys had only gotten on the motorcycle together in order to go pick up a new motorcycle for one of the boys when they were hit by a man driving a truck. Angie said, We never knew why he had hit the boys because his phone records were clear at the time of his accident and it makes sense that he dozed off before he hit the boys.

Trevor said, I have 2 dads in life and please send my love to both of them. He said, you got married after I passed Mom and I didn't miss the wedding. Angie said, wow, yes, I did get re-married after my son passed. I said, when your son talks about your wedding, he is taking me to the casino as well? Angie said that the day of her wedding, she and some friends made a brief stop at a casino. Trevor was going to ensure his Mom knew he was with her on her wedding day. Trevor said, I didn't meet your new husband in life, but I love him and I brought you back together. Trevor said, You wouldn't have made it without him Mom. Angie was in awe because Trevor hadn't met her new husband in life, but she had met her husband back when they were in school and lost touch with him only to be brought back together after Trevor's passing. She had felt her son had brought them to-gether and now he was telling her she was right. Trevor told me that he has a sister and brother that he wants to send his love to as well. Angie said she would be sure to pass his love along to his family for him.

Trevor then gave me a validation that made me giggle. He said Mom put a dorky Christmas Tree out at the accident site in honor of me. He made me feel she had the tree still. Angie said, yes ha ha, I did put one out and she referred to it being like the Charlie Brown Christmas Tree hahaha...

Angie then realized that she had brought the Christmas tree home and she actually Laughed when she realized it is still hanging in Trevor's room.

Trevor made me feel as though there were numerous decorations out for him at the accident site, but he told me the decorations were taken down. Angie said, yes, the city had removed all of the decorations that had been placed in her son's honor and she had wished they would have let her take them down because she would have loved to have saved them.

I said, Trevor tells me you have a Trophy in honor of him? Angie said, OH WOW, I took his car to a car show and it won a trophy after he passed.

Trevor told me that the car means a lot to his brother. Angie said, yes, his brother would love to have the car someday. I said, of course, those things happen in your perfect timing.

Trevor told me that he grew up riding dirt bikes in life. He told me that his Dad helped to start his love for bikes. He wanted to Thank Dad for that love. Angie said, yes, Trevor's Dad gave he and his brother Dirt Bikes as a gift when they were younger and supported the boys love for riding as well.

Trevor wanted me to tell his Mom that he has her horse in Heaven. Trevor said Mom had to make the difficult decision out of love to put this horse down after she had taken a fall and he said, Mom, you did the right thing for her and she is safe with me in Heaven now. It was a relief to hear that her beloved horse is in Heaven with her son as she had always hoped she had made the right decision for her.

Trevor then took me outside and showed me that there is a pond outside at his parent's home. Angie said, Yes, there is a pond outside. I said, he is showing me a big bird on the pond and he says to tell you he sent you the bird. Angie gasped as I said these words because just this week, her husband was taking her across the property on a vehicle and she saw a large blue herring bird on the pond. She said she had her husband stop so she could take pictures of the beautiful bird as they had never seen one like it on the pond. She even went as far as to make noise so that they could get a picture of the beautiful bird in flight. I thought it was beautiful to hear that Angie's attention was caught by her son's beautiful sign of love sent from Heaven in that pond.

There were so many more validations that came through during Angie's reading. Her son did a beautiful job in healing his Mom's broken heart during this reading and filling her with pure love. Trevor is one cool dude in Heaven.

Lisa won her reading in a drawing here on my page. She invited her ex husband to sit in on her reading as well which would turn out to be such a blessing for him as well. You may remember a few days ago that I posted a testimonial from a father of a son in Heaven who had a reading with me. This is their story...

As Lisa called me for their reading, her son in heaven began to come through. As I asked him about his passing, he told me that his passing was sudden and or unexpected. Lisa told me yes, that absolutely makes sense. As I asked her son Garrison to tell me more about his passing, he made me feel as though his passing was drug-related. Garrison told me that he passed due to an overdose. Lisa said yes, Garrison did pass due to an overdose. Garrison showed me that he was at home at the time of his passing. He showed me that his second dad found him when he passed and he wanted to please send his love to his second dad. Garrison also told me that his biological father was listening in with us. Lisa said yes, I have his biological father here with me and she told me that Garrison is correct because his father that lives with her in their home is the one who found him. Garrison wanted his second dad to know that there is nothing more he could have done to save him. He said, I was already passed from my body when I was found. He made me feel as though he passed instantly from heroin overdose.. Garrison said, I got bad drugs. Garrison made me feel as though he struggled for some time with an addiction and he had plenty of support from his parents to get clean. He showed me himself bouncing back and forth between being clean and using and he wanted his family to know that they had done all they could to support his sobriety. Lisa said yes, he passed due to a heroin overdose. She and Garrison's Dad said that Garrison absolutely bounced back and forth between sobriety and using.

Garrison told me that he has a brother as well and he wanted to please send his love to him. Garrison showed me a flash of a young male associated with his brother. Garrison showed me that his brother has a baby boy, and he wanted his brother to know that he held him first in heaven.

Garrison said, please tell my brother that I told his baby all about me and tell my brother thank you for naming him after me. Garrison told me that his brother had given his baby nephew Garrison's middle name and he loved the gesture of love that his brother gave him by honoring him with sharing his name. Lisa said, I knew it! She had felt in her heart that Garrison would have held their grandbaby first before any of them, and Garrison was confirming that. She thought it was beautiful that Garrison knew the baby shares a name with him. Garrison also told me that his brother is going to be taking a trip to the beach and he wanted his brother to know that he will be going with him on that trip. Lisa said yes, our son is going on a trip to the beach and I'm sure he would love to know that his brother is going with him.

Garrison said, my mom has my bracelet and she wears my bracelet in honor of me. Lisa gasped as I said this validation because the very morning of our reading, she came across a bracelet of garrisons that she had never seen before and she was in fact wearing it at the time of our reading. This was Garrison's way of letting his mom know that he was with her from Heaven the day of our reading.

Garrison showed me that he played guitar a little bit in life and he was playing for me in heaven. His mom and dad said yes, he did play around with guitar a little bit. Garrison showed me that his parents honored him with his guitar and made something that they had out on display for him. Lisa said yes, I have a painting that was made with Garrison and his guitar in it and it is out on display. Garrison said, there is actually more than one art piece in honor of me and he told me that his mom is painting in honor of him as well. He showed me that his mom paints flowers in honor of him. Lisa said yes, I am painting and I do paint in honor of my son as well. Lisa went on to say that she has painted flowers in honor of her son also.

Garrison told me that his mom has a tattoo in honor of him. Lisa said yes, I do. Garrison been told me actually mom has two tattoos for me.

Lisa was in awe of this validation because Lisa had a tattoo in honor of Garrison before he passed but she had never told him that it represented him and she has since gotten a tattoo in memory of him since his passing. Garrison was aware that Mom has two tattoos on her skin in honor of him and she loved this validation.

Garrison told me that there were trees planted in honor of him after his passing. His dad said yes, they planted a forest for him LOL.

Garrison told me that his mom had a hummingbird outside and he wanted her to know that he had sent it. Lisa said yes, I just saw a hummingbird recently and this was validation that it was truly from her son.

Garrison told me that his dad has some of his hair saved. Dad said yes, I do have my son's hair saved. Garrison wanted his dad to know that he wasn't missing even the smallest details from heaven.

Garrison told me that one of his plants died and he was laughing at his mom and telling her that she over watered them. His mom said yes, my house is full of plants in honor of Garrison and one of them did die because I'm over-watering them LOL.

Garrison told me that both his mom and his dad wear a necklace that represents him on their neck and he wanted both of them to know that he loves it. His dad said yes, I do have a necklace in honor of my son and Lisa said she does as well. The necklace has Garrison thumb print on it in honor of him.

There were many more validation that came through during Lisa and Michael's reading. Some of those validations I will keep private for their family. The biggest validation of all on this day for each and everyone in their family is that Garrison is filled with love for each and every one of them and watches over them all from heaven.

Sierra contacted me last week to set up a phone reading. She had asked if others could join the phone reading with us and I assured her that it wouldn't be a problem to add others, but to please keep in mind that by adding others to a call, you want to ensure they intend to hear from the same family as you because otherwise, they could have loved ones come through as well. Sierra understood and though she didn't tell me who would be sitting in with her, she told me that someone that will be joining our call was completely skeptical. I assured her that Skeptics were absolutely welcome because I have Heaven behind me. I always have Faith that Heaven will bring the support, Love, and Healing needed to lighten the Heart of a Skeptic.

As I began Sierra's call, I felt as though her Baby Girl was coming through from Heaven. The first validation that little Mia gave me was, "My Daddy is Here!" I said, is your little girl's Daddy sitting with your because she tells me Daddy is here? Sierra said, yes, her Daddy is here with me and that is our baby girl.

I asked little Mia to tell me about her passing. Mia told me that her Grandma was watching her the day that she passed. Mia showed me herself napping peacefully in Grandma's care. Mia then made me feel something that felt like a little blood clot travel up my neck to my brain. Mia said, no one would have seen any symptoms in advance. Mia said, I ate perfectly that day and I was a healthy baby. She said, I didn't give any warnings, so please tell my family not to carry guilt or think they could have done things differently to save me. I said, the Doctors told you this was SIDS? Sierra said, yes, that is what they told us, but they didn't do an autopsy because there was no trauma to our little girl. I said, for your peace of mind, I want you to know that it was an undetectable blood clot. Those words brought peace and comfort to all who were listening to our conversation. Mia wanted her family to know that she had already passed from her little body before she was taken to the Hospital. Sierra said, yes, they said she had passed before she got to the hospital. Mia showed me that her Mommy and Daddy held her in the hospital that day with family surrounding her as well and she wanted them all to know she was with them during that difficult time in spirit.

Mia then told me that her Grandmother was here in the room with her Mommy and Daddy as well. Sierra said, Yes, her Grandma is here. Mia said she loved spening time with her Grandparents. Mia spoke of a tattoo with Angels wings on it in honor of her and Grandma has a tattoo with a little Angel with wings on it with Mia's name.

Mia said, I share a name with my Grandma. Sierra said, yes, Mia's middle name is Nell which is my Mom's middle name.

Mia wanted to start focusing on healing her Daddy and it was apparent to each of us that this little girl was not going to let her Daddy walk away from this conversation without healing his broken heart first. Mia told me that Daddy wears her on his skin. She then corrected me and told me that Daddy has 2 tattoos for Mia. Sierra said, yes, her Daddy does have 2 tattoos for Mia. Mia said, "My Daddy Just realized this is real!" Mia said, My Daddy likes to go offroading. Sierra answered for her husband and said, yes he does. I said, Daddy, your baby girl goes with you when you off-road. Mia then showed me her Daddy on a Motorcycle. Sierra said, yes, her Daddy rides a motorcycle. Mia said, My Daddy had a drink to me and please tell him I was with him when he did. Sierra and her husband seemed confused by this validation, but little Mia knew what she meant and told me to say it a few more times and so I did. I began to feel this was something her Daddy had done in private, not like a toast but she was adamant that her Daddy had a drink for her and he wasn't alone. I heard Sierra's husband speak up in the background and he acknowledged that after their little girl had passed and he left the hospital, he walked straight across the street to a Liquor store for a drink alone.... Mia then began to show me tools for her Daddy and cars and I said, is her Daddy a Mechanic? Sierra said, yes, he is. I said, she shows me Daddy taking apart a car over and over. Sierra laughed because there is a project that her husband has worked on in which he has taken apart the same vehicle a few times ha ha. Mia said, Daddy made something out of metal for me and he welded it too. Sierra said, yes, he made a heart for Mia out of metal and he did weld it as well. Mia was going to let her Daddy know how proud she is to have him and her once Skeptical Daddy was now filled with so much love from his baby girl in Heaven that there was no way he wouldn't know she is with him. I didn't even have to ask who the Skeptic was as we began, Mia knew and she did a beautiful job giving her Daddy Faith.

Mia told me that she is Mommy's #1 Baby Girl. Sierra said, Mia is turning 1 year old this weekend. I said, Mia says you are going to do a balloon release for her? Sierra said, yes we are planning to. Mia then handed me a bouquet of balloons for her Mommy separate from the balloon release validation and made me feel she was just honored with balloons. Sierra said, WOW!!! I Just Drew Balloons for her today at work on a piece of Paper!!!!!!! HOLY CRAP, I had Goose Bumps head to toe as she said these words because her little girl had just made sure Mommy knew she was watching over her.... TODAY! Mia also showed me a hand written note from Mommy and she wanted Mommy to know she had gotten her note. Sierra couldn't place this note I spoke of because she didn't recall ever writing one. Mia didn't sway from the validation and insisted her Mommy had written a note. Again, Sierra couldn't place it, but after the reading, when Sierra sent me the picture of the Balloons she had drawn that day for little Mia, She had also written the words in her own handwriting, " Happy Birthday Baby Girl"

Mia showed me that her Mommy and Daddy had some framed art made in honor of her out on display. Mia said, it isn't just a picture of me and she made me feel it was handmade art. Sierra said, yes, we have her hands and feet made into art on display for her and we framed them in a cage in honor of her.

Mia told me that she has brothers and a sister and she wanted to send her love to them. Mia said that one of her brothers was just recognized with an award at school and she wanted him to know she hadn't missed it. She told me that one of her siblings had just graduated a level in school with a graduation as well. Her Mommy and Daddy said Mia was correct and I just asked that they send Mia's love to her siblings for her.

Mia was then showing me a little fender bender. Mia said it was nothing dangerous but that it had recently happened and she was watching this happen from Heaven. Both Sierra and her husband said they didn't know what Mia was speaking of. But, Mia again was persistent and she kept showing me a little fender bender. I said to the family, "Look, I don't want you to think you are going to hang up the phone with me and that one of you is going to get into an accident because she makes me feel like this already happened and no one was hurt and it was just a little bump into another car?" And then it happened..... Daddy spoke up and said he had bumped into his wife's car in their drive way last week. Hahahahahaha Little Mia was telling on Daddy from Heaven! Hahaha I have to say, that was my favorite validation of the day hahahahah... We all got a good giggle out of Mia's little Tattle.... Because it was filled with Love......

As we were ending the reading, Mia showed me a butterfly fluttering it's wings in my mind's eye. As I described what Mia was showing me, her Daddy spoke up in the background and said, I saw a yellow butterfly today.... Little Mia surely was with her Daddy today too.

Ashley and her husband were just simply going to sit in and listen to their friend Kristie get a reading with me today. Heaven had other plans.

As I was doing Kristie's reading, her husband in heaven was coming through. He gave a few beautiful validations to let Kristie know he is watching over she and their 3 young children and then her husband stepped aside. Kristie has had previous readings with me before. Heaven felt as though there was necessary healing that needed to happen during Kristie's reading today. I was proud of Kristie beyond words for allowing her friend Ashley and Ashley's husband to sit in because this day what about them. Kristie was so loving to think of sharing her time with them during our call.

I told Ashley and her husband that I have a baby boy coming through for them from heaven. This made perfect sense to Ashley and her husband as they have an infant son named Daniel in heaven.

As I asked Daniel to tell me about his passing, he told me that his passing was sudden and or unexpected but that he did not pass at birth. Ashley said yes, that is true. I asked Daniel to tell me more about his passing and he made me feel as though his heart was affected in his passing as well as his breathing. Ashley said, we really never got clear answers as to what happened to our son. I asked Daniel to take me through his passing. Daniel told me that his mommy was with him and trying to help him when she realized something was wrong. Ashley said yes, I was with him and I did try to help him. Daniel took me to the hospital and made me feel as though the hospital was breathing for him. Ashley said yes, they had him on a ventilator system. Little Daniel told me that the hospital was giving very difficult decisions to his mommy and daddy about that ventilator system and he wanted his mommy and daddy to know that they made the right decision because he truly wouldn't have come back from this okay. Ashley said that the doctors really didn't give them much have a choice but more of a suggestion that they take him off of the ventilator. I told Ashley, you did the right thing. Daniel made me feel as though he had heart issues previous to this day that the doctors were aware of. Ashley said yes, he did have heart issues. I said, Daniel tells me that the doctors had talked about doing a surgery on his heart at one point but they never did it and the Dr's put it off. Ashley said yes, they did talk about doing a surgery on his heart and they didn't do the surgery. I said, Daniel tells me that the same doctors that didn't do the surgery are also the doctors that were helping him at the end of his life. Ashley said yes, that is true. I said, that is why the doctors didn't give you much information when it came to his passing because you see little Daniel had the same heart issues that the Dr's knew of before that were affecting him now. Daniel told me that his mommy held him in her arms while he passed to Heaven. Ashley said yes, I did. Daniel then told me that his daddy was there with him as well and showed me that Mommy gave him to Daddy to hold also. Again Ashley and her husband said yes that is true. Daniel then reference to the number 6 and made me feel as though the 6th month or the 6th of a month was significant with his passing. At first, Ashley couldn't place the number six and so I wrote it down and we continued on. Shortly after the reading was complete, I Ashley realized that little Daniels Funeral was held on March 6th.

Daniel told me that the hospital gave his mommy a memorial with his feet. Ashley said yes, they did and she sent me a picture of it and I have to say it is beautiful. Daniel was also talking about Mommy framing pictures of him on that were made in honor of him on an art piece. Ashley said that she has a blanket that has little Daniel's pictures on it and she was going to frame it.

Daniel told me that he shares a name with his daddy and his dad spoke up in the background and said yes he does. I said, he told me that he shares a middle name. Ashley said yes, his first name is his Daddy's middle name. I said daddy he's showing me you with a wrench and he tells me his daddy is a mechanic. His dad softly spoke the words yes I am, in response to his son. I said, your son wants you to know that he's proud of you as his daddy. Daniel also told me that his dad is planning on getting a tattoo in honor of him and he wanted him to know that he loves the idea. His dad said yes, I am planning a tattoo for my son.

Daniel told me that his family did a balloon release in honor of him and he wanted them to know that he was with them as they released these balloons in his honor. He also made me feel as though someone did something with white balloons in honor of him as well. His mom said yes, we did a balloon release in honor of him and he is correct that someone to do something with white balloons in honor of him as well.

Daniel made me feel as though his mommy wears a bracelet for him. At first she thought I meant on her wrist because of course that's where we wear bracelets, but she immediately realised that Daniel was referring to his little bracelet that she wears on a necklace in honor of him and she surely does wear her son's bracelet for him. It was beautiful that her son said this because it's his way of letting his mommy know that he watches over her from heaven and sees how she honors him.

Daniel told me that he has an older sister and he wanted to send his love to her. He told me that his sister is 3 years old and almost 4 and he said that her birthday is coming. Ashley said yes, we have a daughter who is 3, almost 4 years old and her birthday is coming. Daniel said, tell Mommy I'm going to be at my sister's princess birthday party. Ashley seemed to be in awe because she is planning a princess birthday party for her daughter and it was a comfort to know that her daughter's little brother will be there from heaven.

Daniel told me that his mommy has the blanket saved that he was wrapped in at the time that he passed. Ashley said yes, I do have his blanket. Daniel was then showing me that is Mommy saved some of his hair as well and again Ashley said yes I did save my son's hair. Daniel told me that his mommy is getting a tattoo for him also. Ashley said yes, I am planning a tattoo for my son.

Daniel told me that his parents have another baby coming and he wants his parents to know that he met his sibling in heaven. Ashley said yes, I'm pregnant right now. I said your son wants you to know that he's not missing out on his sibling and he wants you to know that he knew his sibling first in heaven. Daniel told me, if it's a boy, my parents are going to name him after me. Ashley said yes we've already spoken about that and we did decide that we would name the baby after Daniel if it is a boy. Daniel said, it's okay Mommy, everything's okay with this baby let go of your worries. I could feel the relief in Ashley's voice as she heard these words from her son because she has been worried about this pregnancy since Daniel passed so unexpectedly.

Kristie received more validations from her husband in between the validation that Ashley and her husband got from Daniel. But I was amazed and proud of Kristie for the way that she set herself aside to bring healing to this family that needed it so much.

Little Daniel is perfect in heaven with God and yes babies do communicate during readings. It was an honor to meet you today little one and I thank you for bringing Mommy and Daddy Healing.

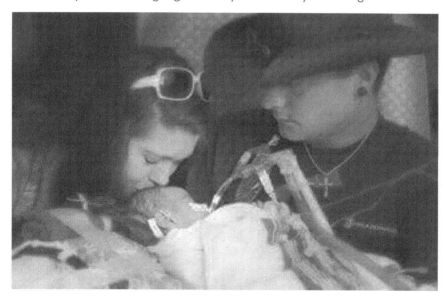

Amy and her daughter called me for a reading yesterday. As we began their reading, I heard a young male in Heaven telling me that Amy is his Mom and that the other young lady on the phone with me is his sister. I asked Amy if she has a Son in Heaven and she said, Yes, My son Ethan passed.

As I asked Ethan to tell me more about his passing, he told me he had taken his own life. Amy said, yes, that is true. I asked Ethan to be more specific about his passing and he made my neck and head feel affected as he restricted my breathing. My heart sank as I had to ask one of the hardest questions I have to ask a parent. I said, "Did he hang himself?". Amy said with a tremble in her voice, yes, he did. Ethan took me to his passing and made me feel his sister had been in the home before he passed. His sister said, yes, I was with him that day until I went to work. I said, he is telling me that he didn't give you any clues that he was going to take his live on this day. His sister said, yes he acted normal and never gave an indication that he would have done this. Ethan went on to show me he had tried taking his life previously with pills unsuccessfully. Mom said, yes, he did try to overdose previously. Ethan was in counseling prior to his passing. His Mom reached out in any way that she could to get him the help he needed. She saw the signs and didn't ignore them. So, my question to Ethan was Why? Ethan made it seem so simple, "I felt Inadequate". Ethan simply felt as though he didn't fit in. Ethan showed me that his Mom was at work, his sister was gone and he took his life by hanging himself. Ethan said that he was completely passed from his body when he showed me that his Dad found him. Ethan said, "My Dad tried to pick me up to help me". Amy said, yes, his Step Dad found him and did try to lift him and help him, but he was already passed. Ethan said, Someone had tried to call him that day and he didn't answer because he was already passed to Heaven. Amy said, yes, one of his friends tried to Snap Chat Ethan and he didn't answer. Ethan said, the guns were locked up in the house just as they should have been which kept me from using a gun. He wanted his Mom to know that she had truly done everything right. Ethan said, Please tell my Mom not to carry guilt anymore for my passing. Ethan was only 13 years old when he took his life. Amy asked that this story be shared to bring awareness to Suicide in hopes of helping someone in Ethan's shoes.

Ethan went on to tell me that he simply felt like he didn't fit in with friends. He said that his mood swings were very up and down. Ethan told me he had written about his emotions on paper and he told me that his Mom has his writings. Amy said, yes, he did write about his emotions and I found the writings after he passed. I said, he tells me that he did not leave a suicide note though? Mom said, no, Ethan didn't leave a note on this day.

Ethan told me that the school honored him in an assembly. Amy said, yes, the school chorus sang his favorite song for him at a school assembly. Ethan showed me that his family just lit something in honor of him as he showed me a lighter and a wick. Amy said, we just lit fireworks in honor of Ethan as a family.

Ethan said, Please tell my Mom I am proud of her for doing Suicide Awareness since my passing. Ethan said, My mom is starting a group to help others. Amy was in Awe that her son knew that she is in fact trying to start a group to support Suicide Awareness in Ethan's Honor.

Ethan took my attention to his sister. He told me his sister just had a relationship milestone? His sister said, wow, I just got Engaged. I said, your brother tells me you are planning an outside wedding. His sister said, yes we are. Ethan showed me that his sister is planning to include him in her wedding and he was extremely excited about this. His sister cried as she said, yes, I am. I wanted Ethan to show me more and so I asked if he would tell me how his sister would be honoring him at her wedding. He showed me his picture walking down the aisle at her wedding. He then showed me an empty seat in honor of him at the wedding and he placed the picture on the empty seat. Ethan's sister's tears could be heard through the phone as she said she has plans for someone to carry her brother's picture down the aisle at her wedding and she also planned an empty seat for her brother at the Alter when she gets married. She was in Awe that her brother knew of her plans. I said, he won't be missing this wedding. Ethan told me that his sister has a bracelet in honor of him that she wears. His sister had tears in her voice as she said, yes, we had a bunch of bracelets made in honor of Ethan and I wear one for him.

Ethan told me that his family is making stickers in honor of him to be placed on cars. He gave me a soccer reference with the stickers as well. His Mom said, yes, we are actually having the stickers made right now and there will be a soccer reference on the stickers because Ethan played Soccer in life.

Mom asked if I could tell her where some of Ethan's old Stuffed animals are that she hasn't been able to find since his passing? I said, when you ask me this, he is showing me a bonfire lol. Amy kind of giggled as she said, "I thought so". She wondered if Ethan had taken them out into the bonfire pit in the back yard and burned them because she knew that Ethan loved a good fire in the back yard and she also knew that he very much disliked those stuffed animals lol. I said, he does tell me that you do have a stuffed animal of his that was up in the top of his closet? His Mom said, yes, I do have an old stuffed animal from when he was a baby that was in the top of his closet and it is in my room now.

Ethan told me that he and his biological Dad hunted and fished with one another in life when he was younger. Mom said, yes they did. Ethan said, but my Step Dad was truly my Father figure in life because my Dad wasn't around when I was growing up. Amy said, yes, that is true as well.

Ethan told me that he had an outdoor trip with his Mom and family right before he passed. Amy said, yes, we took a trip 2 weeks before he passed to the lake as a family. Ethan said, Mom and Dad are planning a trip to the beach and he showed me a barefoot wedding on the beach. Amy said, yes, his Step Dad and I are finally getting married and we are doing it on the beach barefoot in Florida. I said, I want you to know that your son will be there with you on your special day. Ethan then told me that his Mom wears his ashes on her neck in a necklace. As I said this, Amy said, Yes and I had asked Ethan to bring my necklace with his ashes up today during our reading. I said, well, it seems to me that he heard you Mama.

Ethan gave me a reference to the Month of May or #5. Amy said, yes, Ethan just passed in May. I gasped as she said these words because I knew how new this passing was for she and her daughter. I was proud of them beyond belief that they had reached out for a reading so soon in their healing process. I was proud of Ethan for pushing them for this healing.

Ethan told me that his team honored him with a jersey. Amy said, yes, his soccer team got new jerseys just after Ethan passed and since Ethan wasn't there to receive his jersey, the team signed Ethan's Jersey and presented it to me. Ethan then showed me that his team also wore something onto the field for him with their jerseys. His Mom said, yes, they wore bands on their arms in honor of Ethan. Ethan wanted his Mom to know how proud he was of her for attending his team's final game when Ethan was already in Heaven. Ethan said, My team lost the Championship. Amy said, yes, I was there and it was extremely hard to watch his team play without him on the field. Amy said, Ethan is right, the team didn't win the championship because Ethan was the team's Goalie and they truly missed him on the field. Ethan said that the Soccer team had done a moment of silence in honor of him and he loved it. Mom said, yes, The whole organization did a moment of silence for Ethan.

Ethan did a beautiful job of letting his family know that he is still with them and watching over them from Heaven. There were many more validations that came through that I didn't place in the story as well. Ethan was a very normal 13 year old child just trying to feel as though he fit in. What he knows now, is that he fit perfectly and he just didn't see it in life. The outpouring of people who love Ethan has been seen by Ethan in Heaven. If love could have saved him, he would have lived forever. May Ethan's story reach someone in need of saving. May you know that you are enough in this world. Thank you Sweet Ethan for the healing you will bring to so many.

A husband and wife named Margaret and Frank called me last night for a reading. Margaret has been on my page for some time and last night was going to be her first reading with me. Her husband told me as we began the reading that he was very skeptical of this call and I told Frank that I completely understand because truly, until you have an honest experience with a medium it is very hard to wrap your head around this being real. I asked Frank to please have an open heart even if he had a very normal skeptical mind and he agreed that he would.

As we began their reading, I had their son Shane coming through from heaven. As I asked Shane to tell me about his passing, he made me feel as though his passing was sudden and unexpected. Shane told me that his passing was due to some medication that he had taken. His parents said yes, his passing was due to a medication that he had taken that day and he passed in his sleep. I asked Shane to be more specific about this medication and he said to me "I didn't know what the fuck I took". His parents gasped when I said these words because they knew they were true. Shane went on to tell me that he did in fact have an addiction issue earlier in life but made me feel as though he was free from that addiction at the time that he passed. He told me that a friend had given him some medication that in combination with something else in his body caused his passing. His parents said yes, Shane had only had a few drinks and because he has taken this medication, it became a lethal combination but Shane never would have known because they don't believe he knew what he was given by this friend. It could happen to anyone that doesn't know the side effects of a medication they are given. Shane stopped me for a moment during the reading and he wanted me to explain to his parents that he didn't think anything was intentional on his friends part. His friend was just simply trying to help him to feel better and Shane took the responsibility of taking the medication. Shane made it very clear that he did not take his life purposefully but that he was taking some responsibility for taking the medication when he didn't feel good. His parents needed those words from their son. Shane showed me that a male family member found him when he passed but he made me feel as though he was already in heaven when his body was found. His parents told me yes, that is true. Shane told me that his parents weren't home at the time of his passing and he didn't want them to feel guilty for that. He said, please tell them there is nothing they could have done had they been here. Shane made me feel as though his parents were away on vacation when he passed and told me that they had to fly home the next day. Frank explained that he and his wife got the news of their son's passing when they were away on vacation and their scheduled flight was the following day when they returned home. He said it was very difficult to know that their son has passed as they waited through the night for their flight and this was their sons way of letting them know he was with them in that difficult time. As Frank began to engage in speaking to me about the validations that we're coming through, I could feel that his skeptic mind was being filled with love from his son in Heaven.

Shane told me that he has a little girl and he wanted to send his love to her. His mom and dad said yes, he did leave behind a daughter in life. He told me that his daughter is moving up really high in school and she's getting certificates for her grades. His parents told me yes, she is in advanced classes and she does great in school. Shane told me that his daughter moved and that his family doesn't get to see her much and he wanted them to know he is watching over this from heaven. Both Margaret and Frank said this is very true and they miss her so much. I said, he tells me that you are talking about bringing his daughter home to visit for some of her summer time right now. Frank said oh wow, our granddaughter arrives tomorrow for her first visit since our sons passing! Frank was in awe at this point and I could feel his guard drop. Shane said, my parents are planning to share me with my daughter and thinking of ways to share stories and pictures of me with her when she arrives. Margaret said yes, we have already got plans to share her daddy with her. Shane said, my daughter changed her hair and it's cut off shorter than it was before. Frank said yes, she always had long hair and it is much shorter now than before. Shane told me that his parents still have a room for him in their home and he made me feel as though his daughter was in this room as well. Margaret and Frank said yes, we still have his room in our home and his daughters things are still in his room because they shared it when she would come over for her visits when he was living in their home. Shane told me that his little girl is a dancer and he called her his princess. Frank said yes, she was a ballerina and Shane referred to her as his princess. Shane said, my parents are talking about taking my daughter to Disney and please tell them I'm going. Margaret and Frank said yes, we have thought about taking her to Disney World and it was beautiful that their son knew of these plans and plans to attend someday when they go.

Shane told me that he has a brother as well that he wanted to please his love to. He said, my brother wears me on his skin in a gesture of letting his parents know that he sees his brother has a tattoo in honor of him. They said, yes he does. He told me that his brother struggled with an addiction in life as well and he made me feel as though his brother had perhaps even struggle more than him with an addiction but he wanted his brother to know how proud he is of him for the changes he has made in his life. Mom and Dad agreed that Shane's brother has made amazing changes in his life that they are all proud of.

Shane showed me a skateboard and made me feel as though I was hanging it up in honor of him. As I asked his parents about this, they said yes, we hung up his skateboard out in the garage on the wall. Shane said, they were thinking of personalizing my board for me and he jokingly said, don't fuck it up Mom ha ha. Margaret laughed as I said these words because she could feel her son's a spunky personality coming through in the reading and she had in fact thought of having it personalized but she knew how important his board was to him so she hadn't made any changes to it LOL.

Shane told me that his mom passed one of his hats down to one of his really good friends and he wanted to thank her for this. Mom said yes, I did pass one of his hats down to one of his really good friends.

Shane told me that he shares a name in life with an older male on Dad's side of the family. He said, I need to salute the man that I was named after and made me feel as though this man was in the military and life. Frank said yes, he was given the middle name of my brother and my brother was in the military. Frank wanted his dad to know that he's watching over his brother from Heaven because he made me feel as though he had recently had some medical treatment. He said, please tell my uncle that I am at his side and watching over him from heaven. Frank found comfort in those words because his brother had in fact had some recent medical issues and it was nice to know that his brother was being watched over by his son in Heaven.

Shane made a gesture of slapping a huge birthday cake down in front of my mind's eye and said tell them Happy Birthday from Heaven! As I said this, Frank told me that he and his wife had both just celebrated their birthdays this month and Margaret said, I even had a surprise birthday party for Frank. This was Shane's way of saying that he was with them for their birthdays.

Shane told me that his mom writes letters and notes to him and he wanted her to know that he gets her notes. Margaret said yes, I do. Shane also told me that Mom wears a necklace in honor of him as well and Mom said yes I do wear a necklace for him. Shane said to me that he passed down a necklace as well and he told me the word hemp. Margaret said yes, I have a necklace of my sons and it hangs up in honor of him and it is made of hemp!

Shane said, my mom lights candles in honor of me and please tell her that I love the candles. Margaret said wow, I have a candle lit for him in front of his dad and I right now. She said, can he see us right now? I said yes he absolutely can. Margaret said, does he know what I'm holding in my hand for him? I explained to Margaret that I didn't want to stress about asking him this question but hopefully he would bring it up himself. At this point, Shane made me feel as though I was holding a coin in honor of him that used to be his. As I said these words, Margaret said, I'm holding his coin, that is what I'm holding! That I wondered if he saw! Shane said, this is a special coin of mine and it was the first coin. Margaret was in awe because she was holding her son's sobriety coin and it was his first coin and he was so proud of it!

Shane told me that he and his dad had gone shooting together but only one time and he made me feel as though it was cool as hell. At first, Frank couldn't remember going shooting with his son and then he recalled taking his son just one time to the shooting range and they did have an amazing time. It was something he had almost forgotten about but his son surely haven't forgotten that one-on-one time with his dad.

I knew that Shane was funky and fun from all of the fun cuss words that he had given me throughout the reading lol, but this next validation had me pretty confused haha. All I could do was explain what he was showing me in my mind's eye to his parents. I said, is there a reason that your son is showing me himself doing a front flip with a watermelon on his head? LOL! His parents both laughed hysterically (Thank God because it was a bit off the wall to throw that out during a reading) as they said "That's our son!" Evidently he loved the show Jackass in life and he would do some of the craziest stunts in honor of that show with some of his friends haha and we all got a good laugh out of this one for sure.

Shane was telling me about the dogs that had passed within their family because he had them at his side in heaven and he gave a description of a few of them that was on point. He also wanted to send his love to the little dog that was still living with his parents he said, it has snotting issues haha. His dad said he has, this breed does have snorting issues haha.

The next validation that came through made my heart shine. He said, "Dad doesn't think this is bullshit now!" Ha ha ha... Frank said, no I don't, he's right. Those words rang in my soul. Shane hadn't just healed his Mama's Heart, he had also given his Dad new faith and healed his Dad's broken heart as well.

As I said before, I can't explain to you what it feels like to connect a parent with a child in heaven. But, it is a feeling I will never forget. Way to go Shane!

Dawn was the winner last week on my page of my first of the month drawing for a free phone reading giveaway. Last night, Dawn and I were on the phone with one another for that reading. She asked her cousin and her cousin's daughter to sit in with her for support and it it was a beautiful experience for all three ladies.

Dawn's mom began to come through as we began her reading. Mom told me that she had been sick at the end of her life. She gave me a reference to a chronic lung disease and I asked Dawn if her mom had COPD because mom made me feel as though this is what caused her passing. Dawn said yes my mom had COPD and that was the reason she passed. I began to laugh at the next reference that her feisty mom showed me. I love it when their personality comes through right at the beginning of a reading. Mom showed me herself dragging an oxygen tank around in life with a cigarette in the other hand and made me feel as though that oxygen wasn't going to keep her from her cigarettes LOL. Dawn yelled out through her tears, that's my mom!

Mom told me that Dawn had taken good care of her when she was sick. She wanted to thank her daughter for all that she had done for her. Dawn said yes I did help to take care of my mom. Mom showed me that Dawn had come and stayed with her at the end of her life and she wanted to thank her for being there as she was. Dawn again said yes, I stayed with her when she was sick to help out. Mom showed me that she had a live-in boyfriend herself but she said that her daughter took much better care of her LOL. Dawn laughed at this and said boy isn't that the truth LOL.

Mom took me to the day of her passing, she took me to a care facility and made me feel as though she was surrounded by her family. She told me that her son was at her side and she made me feel as though there was a sister at her side as well. Dawn said yes, it was a sister-in-law. I explained to them that the in-law part of that sister comments goes out the window in heaven because we are all truly just family in Heaven. I just love how that works! Mom said, I waited for Dawn to arrive. Dawn cried as I said those words because her Mom had waited for her to get there before she passed to Heaven. Mom wanted to Thank Dawn for telling her, "It's okay Mom, I'm here and you can go to Heaven now." As I said these words to Dawn, you could hear the tears coming through the phone. Dawn said, that is exactly what I told her when I got there. I told Dawn how proud I was of her for having the strength to give those beautiful words to her mom. Her mom appreciated them more than she will ever know. Mom said, Thank you for holding my hand to heaven. Dawn cried as she said, yes I did hold her hand to heaven.

Mom told me that her ex-husband which is Dawn's father is still living. She made me feel as though she wanted to send a thank you to him. She said, please tell my ex-husband thank you for showing love and support for me through our children. Mom made me feel as though her ex had put aside the differences they may have had with one another in life and he supported his children through mom's loss and she was very proud of him for that and wanted to send her love. Dawn said wow, this is really overwhelming and yes my dad did support as kids through it just as mom says he did.

Mom told me that she has multiple Sons and she wanted to send her love to each of them. She said that one of her sons is into shooting guns. She made me feel as though one of her sons may have a distance from the family and she wanted to send her love to him as well.

Mom told me that she went mudding in life with the girls that were listening in on the call. Dawn's cousin spoke up and said yes, we did go mudding with her when we were younger.

Mom was then showing me cinnamon rolls?! It was a random validation and I almost didn't say it but I thought well who am I to question heaven and so I said why the heck is Mom showing me cinnamon rolls? I wasn't sure if she was known for baking them in life and the girls abruptly said oh no, Mom couldn't bake at all LOL. I said, then there must be something to do with cinnamon rolls today that's happened? She makes me feel as though the cinnamon rolls are important today. Dawn's cousin said, my Son's fiancé called my son today and told him that she's going to be making cinnamon rolls for him. Mom made me feel as though she was very close to this young man in life and she didn't want to leave him out and this was her way of letting him know that she was a part of their conversation. As silly as cinnamon rolls may of sounded to me, I'm sure they certainly didn't seem silly to this young man who was close to her in life.

Mom said, I need to please acknowledge my daughter's son. At this point, mom showed me herself holding two babies in heaven for Dawn. Dawn said yes, I gave birth to a son who passed. Dawn's son came through briefly and he told me that he was born in the middle of her pregnancy. He said, they gave you an opportunity to see me but you didn't get an opportunity to hold me and please know I love you very much. Again the tears flowed in Dawn's voice as she acknowledged that her son was correct. I said, your son tells me that he has a sister with him in heaven as well. At first Dawn said she wasn't sure what I was speaking of. I said, you must have miscarried another baby because he's showing me another baby with him in heaven and she said oh yes! I did I miscarry another baby early in a pregnancy. I said yes and she's a little girl and she's with her brother. Dawn gasped through her tears and I could feel the healing in that moment that was given to her by her babies in Heaven who are with her Mom.

Mom made a gesture of placing a necklace around my neck. Dawn said yes, we buried Mom with her necklace. Mom told me that Dawn has a ring of hers and Dawn said yes, I do. Mom got even more specific and told me that dawn has a mother's ring with multiple colored stones in that was hers as well. Dawn said, Wow, yes I do have that ring!

Mom made me feel that although Dawn Didn't get much of Mom's things from her ex-boyfriend that she was living with at the time of her passing but she did get the important things. Dawn said yes that is true. Mom told me that Dawn had trouble getting some of Mom's clothing from this man after her passing as a keepsake. Mom said "What was he gonna do,

Wear the Shit?! LOL". Dawn laughed as I said those words because she said she had asked those exact same words herself haha.

Mom made me feel as though Dawn had some vehicle issues that Mom was responsible for it she was giggling about this. She was taking me to the radio on the vehicle and she then said, you're welcome. Dawn laughed as I said this because in her previous vehicle, after Mom passed, the Bluetooth would get stuck on and she couldn't turn it off! She knew it was Mom! She said it happened so much that she traded a vehicle in and got a new vehicle. I repeated the words, mom says your welcome LOL. Evidently mom was taking responsibility for the new car that Dawn was driving now ha ha.

There were many more of validations that came through during this reading both for Dawn and the ladies who joined her for this reading. But the healing that happened in this reading was immeasurable. Dawn shared the validations that mom sent with the others in the family that mom had brought up and she said they were very excited to hear from her. I was blessed to be a part of their healing.

A woman named Vicki reached out to me last week and said that she wanted to gift a reading to a friend. I am always in awe of such a beautiful gift because I know the impact that gift will have on the person who received it. Vicki told her friend Sara of the gift and Sara and I worked out a day and time for her reading. Sara wasn't familiar with me prior to Vicki telling her of this gift and I am always humbled by the trust I am given when doing a reading for someone who really doesn't know much about me. Last night, Sara and I got on the phone with one another. It only took moments of my opening speech before Heaven was interrupting and I knew in that Moment why it was the Vicki had given such a beautiful gift.

I had a little girl stepping through from Heaven. She told me that her passing was sudden and unexpected. Sara said, yes, that makes sense. The little girl in Heaven then said, That is my Mommy. Sara was taken back as I said these words and she said, yes, that is my Allie. As I began to ask Allie how she passed, Allie said, I shouldn't have been where I was. Allie then showed me that she had pulled a drawer out in her bedroom and began to climb on the drawer. Allie said she wanted to change the Disney Channel on the TV. Allie then made me feel as though she had a fall and she had taken an impact to her head in that fall. Allie said, please tell my Mommy that I didn't suffer and I passed instantly to Heaven when it hit me. Sara spoke through tears as I said these words as little 2 year old Allie was in her bedroom watching TV for only a few moments when she had decided to change the channel herself like a big girl without asking for help. Allie had indeed pulled out a drawer to climb on the furniture and as she did, it and the TV came tumbling down on Allie taking her to Heaven instantly. Allie showed me that her Mommy came in and found her when she heard the crash. She said, "Mommy, there is nothing more you could have done to save me because I was already in Heaven." Sara understood those words, though they weren't easy for her to understand as a Mom. Allie told me that her Daddy wasn't home at the time of the accident and she said, Mommy needs to let go of the guilt she is carrying, please tell Mommy to Hand it to God. Sara responded with tears that she just didn't know how to do that, though she knows in her heart it was an accident. I said, Allie doesn't want to leave anything behind for you and her Daddy but a Smile when you think of her. Sara was going to try to gather up the guilt within her soul and hand it to God as little Allie asked.

Allie said, someone just named a baby after me! Sara said, WOW, we know someone who just recently had a baby and though they didn't do it intentionally, the baby has a shared name with Allie and we were just talking about this. I said, you see, Allie wants you to know she isn't missing out on even the little things.

Allie told me she has a Brother and a sister. Allie said, there are 3 of us children. Sara said, yes, I have 3 children and Allie does have a brother and a sister. Allie took me to her funeral and told me that her Mommy and Daddy placed a little white stuffed animal with her in her casket. Sara again was taken back at Allie's detail because they had placed a little white stuffed animal with her. Allie then told me that her brother and sister placed items with her as well. Sara said, yes, they did. I actually asked if Allie would show me what her brother and sister placed with her as well so that I could relay it to her Mommy and Allie said, "They colored pictures for me." Sara said, YES, her brother and sister had colored pictures for her and they placed them with her, Wow....

Allie said, my sister references me as an angel and she draws me as an angel. Sara said that their daughter references Allie as her Angel and she did in fact draw a picture of Allie as an Angel as well. Allie said, My brother was just recognized at school with an award and she giggled because she said it was a shock that her brother got an award for anything in school. Sara laughed and said that their son had just received an award at school and when he got it, she and her husband were surprised and of course proud when he got an award because they didn't expect it or have any idea what it could have been for ha ha.

Allie told me that she was just a little rambunxious girl that would love to play outside in her panties and get dirty. She said, I was a little Tomboy in life. Sara said, yes, that is exactly my little girl.

Allie then said, My Mommy marches in honor of me. When they give me this validation it tells me that Mommy is doing something in honor of Allie to help others who may be in her shoes. Allie said, Mommy is trying to save other children like me. Allie then said, Tell my Mommy that I have the little boy here in Heaven who passed like I did. Allie said, My Mommy knows his parents and he is perfect here in Heaven just like Me. Sara didn't know what to say as Allie said these words because Allie has started an organization in honor of Allie that is called "Anchoring For Allie". Sara said it is to bring awareness for parents to anchor furniture when they have small children in the home. Sara said, I do know exactly which little boy she is speaking of and I have spoken with his parents, Wow.....

Allie told me that her Mommy has a tattoo in honor of her. She said Mommy has my name on the tattoo. Sara said, yes her initials of her name are on the tattoo. Allie said, Daddy has a tattoo on his arm in honor of me and Sara said, yes, her Daddy does have a tattoo on his arm. Allie told me that Mommy wears wings in honor of her as well and Sara said, yes, I have a necklace with wings in honor of Allie. Allie then made a heart with her fingers in the air and Sara said, my tattoo in honor of Allie is a Heart.

Allie told me that people are putting pretty pinwheels at her grave and she wanted to Thank Them. She said Mommy has a Pretty Wind Chime in honor of her that was gifted by a female in the family that she wanted to send her love to. Sara said, yes, I have the wind chime and it was gifted by her Aunt.

Allie interrupted me when I was speaking and wrapped a blanket around me. I explained this gesture to Sara and she said, OH WOW, I Just wrapped up in Allie's blanket while we were talking just now! Allie wanted Mommy to know she could see her in that moment.

Allie then started to sing the song "One Call Away". She told me that she keeps sending that song to her Mommy. Sara said, oh I hear that song all of the time and I always cry when I hear it and so I turn it off but it keeps popping up and I didn't realize it was my little girl sending it. I laughed as she said this and said, it is okay Sara, people miss beautiful signs they are given quite often and I'm sure you won't be changing the channel next time. Sara said, oh no, I will be listening.

Allie said, "Daddy's Coming Home!" Sara said, Oh my Gosh, I think I just heard my husband pulling up to the house from work!!!! Little Allie wasn't going to leave her precious Daddy out......

Allie did a beautiful Job healing her Mommy. I don't know that Vicki knew the depth of the gift she had given to Sara, but I am sure after she reads this, she will have some idea. Sara continues to try to bring awareness to other parents in honor of Allie in hopes of saving other children from a similar passing. She sent me a page that she created in honor of that awareness for Allie and I will include it at the bottom of this story. Allie, you are such a beautiful and amazing soul who will touch so many in this life.

https://m.facebook.com/anchoringforallie/

A woman named Vicki reached out to me last week and said that she wanted to gift a reading to a friend. I am always in awe of such a beautiful gift because I know the impact that gift will have on the person who received it. Vicki told her friend Sara of the gift and Sara and I worked out a day and time for her reading. Sara wasn't familiar with me prior to Vicki telling her of this gift and I am always humbled by the trust I am given when doing a reading for someone who really doesn't know much about me. Last night, Sara and I got on the phone with one another. It only took moments of my opening speech before Heaven was interrupting and I knew in that Moment why it was the Vicki had given such a beautiful gift.

I had a little girl stepping through from Heaven. She told me that her passing was sudden and unexpected. Sara said, yes, that makes sense. The little girl in Heaven then said, That is my Mommy. Sara was taken back as I said these words and she said, yes, that is my Allie. As I began to ask Allie how she passed, Allie said, I shouldn't have been where I was. Allie then showed me that she had pulled a drawer out in her bedroom and began to climb on the drawer. Allie said she wanted to change the Disney Channel on the TV. Allie then made me feel as though she had a fall and she had taken an impact to her head in that fall. Allie said, please tell my Mommy that I didn't suffer and I passed instantly to Heaven when it hit me. Sara spoke through tears as I said these words as little 2 year old Allie was in her bedroom watching TV for only a few moments when she had decided to change the channel herself like a big girl without asking for help. Allie had indeed pulled out a drawer to climb on the furniture and as she did, it and the TV came tumbling down on Allie taking her to Heaven instantly. Allie showed me that her Mommy came in and found her when she heard the crash. She said, "Mommy, there is nothing more you could have done to save me because I was already in Heaven." Sara understood those words, though they weren't easy for her to understand as a Mom. Allie told me that her Daddy wasn't home at the time of the accident and she said, Mommy needs to let go of the guilt she is carrying, please tell Mommy to Hand it to God. Sara responded with tears that she just didn 't know how to do that, though she knows in her heart it was an accident. I said, Allie doesn't want to leave anything behind for you and her Daddy but a Smile when you think of her. Sara was going to try to gather up the guilt within her soul and hand it to God as little Allie asked.

Allie said, someone just named a baby after me! Sara said, WOW, we know someone who just recently had a baby and though they didn't do it intentionally, the baby has a shared name with Allie and we were just talking about this. I said, you see, Allie wants you to know she isn't missing out on even the little things.

Allie told me she has a Brother and a sister. Allie said, there are 3 of us children. Sara said, yes, I have 3 children and Allie does have a brother and a sister. Allie took me to her funeral and told me that her

Mommy and Daddy placed a little white stuffed animal with her in her casket. Sara again was taken back at Allie's detail because they had placed a little white stuffed animal with her. Allie then told me that her brother and sister placed items with her as well. Sara said, yes, they did. I actually asked if Allie would show me what her brother and sister placed with her as well so that I could relay it to her Mommy and Allie said, "They colored pictures for me." Sara said, YES, her brother and sister had colored pictures for her and they placed them with her, Wow....

Allie said, my sister references me as an angel and she draws me as an angel. Sara said that their daughter references Allie as her Angel and she did in fact draw a picture of Allie as an Angel as well. Allie said, My brother was just recognized at school with an award and she giggled because she said it was a shock that her brother got an award for anything in school. Sara laughed and said that their son had just received an award at school and when he got it, she and her husband were surprised and of course proud when he got an award because they didn't expect it or have any idea what it could have been for ha ha.

Allie told me that she was just a little rambunxious girl that would love to play outside in her panties and get dirty. She said, I was a little Tomboy in life. Sara said, yes, that is exactly my little girl.

Allie then said, My Mommy marches in honor of me. When they give me this validation it tells me that Mommy is doing something in honor of Allie to help others who may be in her shoes. Allie said, Mommy is trying to save other children like me. Allie then said, tell my Mommy that I have the little boy here in Heaven who passed like I did. Allie said, My Mommy knows his parents and he is perfect here in Heaven just like Me. Sara didn't know what to say as Allie said these words because Allie has started an organization in honor of Allie that is called "Anchoring For Allie". Sara said it is to bring awareness for parents to anchor furniture when they have small children in the home. Sara said, I do know exactly which little boy she is speaking of and I have spoken with his parents, Wow.....

Allie told me that her Mommy has a tattoo in honor of her. She said Mommy has my name on the tattoo. Sara said, yes her initials of her name are on the tattoo. Allie said, Daddy has a tattoo on his arm in honor of me and Sara said, yes, her Daddy does have a tattoo on his arm. Allie told me that Mommy wears wings in honor of her as well and Sara said, yes, I have a necklace with wings in honor of Allie. Allie then made a heart with her fingers in the air and Sara said, my tattoo in honor of Allie is a Heart.

Allie told me that people are putting pretty pinwheels at her grave and she wanted to Thank Them. She said Mommy has a Pretty Wind Chime in honor of her that was gifted by a female in the family that she wanted to send her love to. Sara said, yes, I have the wind chime and it was gifted by her Aunt.

Allie interrupted me when I was speaking and wrapped a blanket around me. I explained this gesture to Sara and she said, OH WOW, I Just wrapped up in Allie's blanket while we were talking just now! Allie wanted Mommy to know she could see her in that moment.

Allie then started to sing the song "One Call Away". She told me that she keeps sending that song to her Mommy. Sara said, oh I hear that song all of the time and I always cry when I hear it and so I turn it off but it keeps popping up and I didn't realize it was my little girl sending it. I laughed as she said this and said, it is okay Sara, people miss beautiful signs they are given quite often and I'm sure you won't be changing the channel next time. Sara said, oh no, I will be listening.

Allie said, "Daddy's Coming Home!" Sara said, Oh my Gosh, I think I just heard my husband pulling up to the house from work!!!! Little Allie wasn't going to leave her precious Daddy out......

Allie did a beautiful Job healing her Mommy. I don't know that Vicki knew the depth of the gift she had given to Sara, but I am sure after she reads this, she will have some idea. Sara continues to try to bring awareness to other parents in honor of Allie in hopes of saving other children from a similar passing. She sent me a page that she created in honor of that awareness for Allie and I will include it at the bottom of this story. Allie, you are such a beautiful and amazing soul who will touch so many in this life.

https://m.facebook.com/anchoringforallie/

A woman named Vicki reached out to me last week and said that she wanted to gift a reading to a friend. I am always in awe of such a beautiful gift because I know the impact that gift will have on the person who received it. Vicki told her friend Sara of the gift and Sara and I worked out a day and time for her reading. Sara wasn't familiar with me prior to Vicki telling her of this gift and I am always humbled by the trust I am given when doing a reading for someone who really doesn't know much about me. Last night, Sara and I got on the phone with one another. It only took moments of my opening speech before Heaven was interrupting and I knew in that Moment why it was the Vicki had given such a beautiful gift.

I had a little girl stepping through from Heaven. She told me that her passing was sudden and unexpected. Sara said, yes, that makes sense. The little girl in Heaven then said, That is my Mommy. Sara was taken back as I said these words and she said, yes, that is my Allie. As I began to ask Allie how she passed, Allie said, I shouldn't have been where I was. Allie then showed me that she had pulled a drawer out in her bedroom and began to climb on the drawer. Allie said she wanted to change the Disney Channel on the TV. Allie then made me feel as though she had a fall and she had taken an impact to her head in that fall. Allie said, please tell my Mommy that I didn't suffer and I passed instantly to Heaven when it hit me. Sara spoke through tears as I said these words as little 2 year old Allie was in her bedroom watching TV for only a few moments when she had decided to change the channel herself like a big girl without asking for help. Allie had indeed pulled out a drawer to climb on the furniture and as she did, it and the TV came tumbling down on Allie taking her to Heaven instantly. Allie showed me that her Mommy came in and found her when she heard the crash. She said, "Mommy, there is nothing more you could have done to save me because I was already in Heaven." Sara understood those words, though they weren't easy for her to understand as a Mom. Allie told me that her Daddy wasn't home at the time of the accident and she said, Mommy needs to let go of the guilt she is carrying, please tell Mommy to Hand it to God. Sara responded with tears that she just didn't know how to do that, though she knows in her heart it was an accident. I said, Allie doesn't want to leave anything behind for you and her Daddy but a Smile when you think of her. Sara was going to try to gather up the guilt within her soul and hand it to God as little Allie asked.

Allie said, someone just named a baby after me! Sara said, WOW, we know someone who just recently had a baby and though they didn't do it intentionally, the baby has a shared name with Allie and we were just talking about this. I said, you see, Allie wants you to know she isn't missing out on even the little things.

Allie told me she has a Brother and a sister. Allie said, there are 3 of us children. Sara said, yes, I have 3 children and Allie does have a brother and a sister. Allie took me to her funeral and told me that her Mommy and Daddy placed a little white stuffed animal with her in her casket. Sara again was taken back at Allie's detail because they had placed a little white stuffed animal with her. Allie then told me that her brother and sister placed items with her as well. Sara said, yes, they did. I actually asked if Allie would show me what her brother and sister placed with her as well so that I could relay it to her Mommy and Allie said, "They colored pictures for me." Sara said, YES, her brother and sister had colored pictures for her and they placed them with her, Wow....

Allie said, my sister references me as an angel and she draws me as an angel. Sara said that their daughter references Allie as her Angel and she did in fact draw a picture of Allie as an Angel as well. Allie said, My brother was just recognized at school with an award and she giggled because she said it was a shock that her brother got an award for anything in school. Sara laughed and said that their son had just received an award at school and when he got it, she and her husband were surprised and of course proud when he got an award because they didn't expect it or have any idea what it could have been for ha ha.

Allie told me that she was just a little rambunxious girl that would love to play outside in her panties and get dirty. She said, I was a little Tomboy in life. Sara said, yes, that is exactly my little girl.

Allie then said, My Mommy marches in honor of me. When they give me this validation it tells me that Mommy is doing something in honor of Allie to help others who may be in her shoes. Allie said, Mommy is trying to save other children like me. Allie then said, Tell my Mommy that I have the little boy here in Heaven who passed like I did. Allie said, My Mommy knows his parents and he is perfect here in Heaven just like Me. Sara didn't know what to say as Allie said these words because Allie has started an organization in honor of Allie that is called "Anchoring For Allie". Sara said it is to bring awareness for parents to anchor furniture when they have small children in the home. Sara said, I do know exactly which little boy she is speaking of and I have spoken with his parents, Wow.....

Allie told me that her Mommy has a tattoo in honor of her. She said Mommy has my name on the tattoo. Sara said, yes her initials of her name are on the tattoo. Allie said, Daddy has a tattoo on his arm in honor of me and Sara said, yes, her Daddy does have a tattoo on his arm. Allie told me that Mommy wears wings in honor of her as well and Sara said, yes, I have a necklace with wings in honor of Allie. Allie then made a heart with her fingers in the air and Sara said, my tattoo in honor of Allie is a Heart.

Allie told me that people are putting pretty pinwheels at her grave and she wanted to Thank Them. She said Mommy has a Pretty Wind Chime in honor of her that was gifted by a female in the family that she wanted to send her love to. Sara said, yes, I have the wind chime and it was gifted by her Aunt.

Allie interrupted me when I was speaking and wrapped a blanket around me. I explained this gesture to Sara and she said, OH WOW, I Just wrapped up in Allie's blanket while we were talking just now! Allie wanted Mommy to know she could see her in that moment.

Allie then started to sing the song "One Call Away". She told me that she keeps sending that song to her Mommy. Sara said, oh I hear that song all of the time and I always cry when I hear it and so I turn it off but it keeps popping up and I didn't realize it was my little girl sending it. I laughed as she said this and said, it is okay Sara, people miss beautiful signs they are given quite often and I'm sure you won't be changing the channel next time. Sara said, oh no, I will be listening.

Allie said, "Daddy's Coming Home!" Sara said, Oh my Gosh, I think I just heard my husband pulling up to the house from work!!!! Little Allie wasn't going to leave her precious Daddy out......

Allie did a beautiful Job healing her Mommy. I don't know that Vicki knew the depth of the gift she had given to Sara, but I am sure after she reads this, she will have some idea. Sara continues to try to bring awareness to other parents in honor of Allie in hopes of saving other children from a similar passing. She sent me a page that she created in honor of that awareness for Allie and I will include it at the bottom of this story. Allie, you are such a beautiful and amazing soul who will touch so many in this life.

https://m.facebook.com/anchoringforallie/

8

Poems From Heaven

People are always asking me to put my poems in a book so that they may look back on them when they need them most. So, I think that each book I write will always have a Poem chapter. This chapter is filled with the poems I have written between publishing my last book, Looking Into The Windows Of Heaven, and now. Each poem is inspired by Heaven. If you feel your loved one within these words, it is not by chance. May the words in these poems resonate within your soul for healing.

I Brush Against You Softly

I brush against you softly
As I wipe away your tear
Don't cry for me in Heaven
I am well, I'm fine, I'm here
I whisper into your ear
That I'm wrapped inside your soul
My love for you won't change
I am the half that makes you whole
I send you signs from Heaven
So you won't keep missing me
Those signs surround you every day
My signs sometimes you may not see
If some days you cannot feel me
It doesn't mean I am not there
I am the sun upon your face
I am the wind within your hair
Don't feel bad when you are happy
For that is what I want for you
And please just smile for me each day
For I am here to see you through
It's simply not your time to go
But, my soul's journey there was through
And someday we will meet again
I'll be in Heaven to meet you
So for now go on, live, be happy
Please chase your dreams let go of fears
And I'll be here cheering you on
As you live out your life's last years

Pinkys Up As You Slide In

My trip to Heaven was pretty sweet
Yes, I arrived here with some flair
I slid in sideways screaming yee haw
With my pinkys up in the air
Life wasn't meant to be so boring
And oh some living I have done
They still tell stories of me now
Yes, I'm known as a crazy one
I lived each day there to its fullest
And each night my heart had a smile
I hope I blessed you with sweet memories
As I lived life in my own style
I hope I left you with some laughs
As I shared with you my life's years
Please don't just focus that I'm gone
I ask that you don't cry those tears
You see, I'm right here at your side
So raise your glass, remember me
Let's toast to my amazing life
I'm perfect here, someday you'll see
So when your journey there is over
Yes, I'll be here to see you again
But please just do me one small favor
Pinky's up as you slide in

FARA GIBSON

Hey Mommy I'm Right Here With You

Hey Mommy I'm right here with you
And God's here with me too
I know you want to hold me
Just like you used to do
But I'm perfect up in Heaven now
So please don't be so sad
I love you through each day you live
And cherish times we had
Hey Mommy it's not sad up here
We're happy every day
There is no sadness, pain, or fear
They've all been washed away
I know you talk to me at night
As tears fall on your face
I hear you as you whisper
"Please let me feel your embrace"
Hey Mommy I'll be at your side
As you live your life through
And Mommy when your life is done
I'll be waiting for you
So live life to its fullest now
So I can watch you smile
And make memories with others there
That will last their hearts a while
Hey Mommy I'll be right here
Watching you continue on
And Hey Mommy I sure love you
Please don't think of me as gone

As Those Raindrops Fell Out Of The Sky

If all of the love up in heaven
Showered down right upon you and I
We would feel that our loved ones are with us
As those raindrops fell out of the sky
If all of the stars in the night sky
Could speak as they shined there so bright
Then we'd hear the sweet words of our loved ones
And we wouldn't feel lonely at night
If the waves in the ocean brought healing
As each wave crashed upon the seashore
We would sit with our toes in the water
And we just wouldn't cry anymore
When the wind blows, if we could feel their touch
Brush against us as we live our years
We would know that they're standing at our side
As they wipe away all of our tears
As we walk through this world filled with beauty
God we ask you, help us feel their love
For their journey's in Heaven with you now
As they watch over us from Above

FARA GIBSON

For We Are Only Passing Through

Our true home is in Heaven
And we are simply traveling through
This life is just a chapter
In the book of life for me and you
We travel through with others
Who may get lost along the way
We may be lessons for each other
While crossing mountains every day
Perhaps those who began our path
Have simply taken different trails
And now they've blessed us with more room
To throw our bow lines, set our sails
You see, this life is not complex
Like our minds make it out to be
We're all a part of God's pure love
Yes, God Exists in You and Me
For now we're only passing through
We learn and grow along the way
We find our strength throughout our trials
As we live life through trials each day
Then someday we'll return to Heaven
And we'll look back on all we've done
We will be proud of strength we gained
And know how we affected everyone
So when you reach your last life step
Of this life shared by me and you
Your next step will be walked in Heaven
For we are only passing through

Do You Feel Me Standing Next To You

Do you feel me standing next to you
As the tears stream down your face
Heaven is right here all around you
I'm perfect now in God's embrace
Do you feel me standing next to you
Hoping that you will sense me near
I know you love me and you miss me
Your words and thoughts to me I hear
Do you feel me standing next to you
As you ask why I had to go
You see, I'm standing here right next to you
I'm closer than you truly know
Do you feel me standing next to you
As your sweet life there carries on
Just know I'm proud of you from Heaven
I'm not missing out, I am not gone
Do you feel me standing next to you
As you begin to chase your dreams
Lets catch those dreams of yours together
Heaven's not as far as it seems
Do you feel me standing next to you
When you ask God to take you please
You see, it just isn't your time
I comfort you with gentle breeze
Do you feel me standing next to you
One day you'll stand here next to me
For now please live life to its fullest
And standing next to you I'll be

Remember Me

Remember me within your laughter
I am the corners of your smile
Though it is hard since I'm in Heaven
You know that crying's not my style
Remember me within your footsteps
I will be right here at your side
Please go wherever your heart leads you
You see, my spirit never died
Remember me as you embrace life
Please honor me in all you do
Though you can't see me with your eyes now
Just know that I now live through you
Remember me as you lie sleeping
I'll sometimes see you in your dreams
You see, those dreams are truly visits
We're truly closer than it seems
Remember me up in the star light
Each time you gaze upon the sky
Just speak to me because I hear you
No need to keep asking God why
Remember me for all my love
And my sweet memories left behind
My legacy will never fade
For our two souls are intertwined
Remember me on your life's path
Until your life on Earth is through
And on that day, I'll be right there
And yes, I will Remember You

You Are Not Alone

You're not alone in silence
You're not alone in Fear
You're not alone, I'm at your side
I'm well, I'm Fine, I'm Here
I know that you still miss me
I know that you still care
I know your one and only wish
Is that you still had me there
I see the days you struggle
I see you cry at night
If only I could help you see
I'm perfectly alright
Our life is but a journey
A path that has no end
I wish that I could help you see
I'm just around the bend
For Heaven is a Beautiful place
A place that's filled with love
A part of our sweet journey
Where our Souls meet up above
But it isn't way up in the sky
So look for me no more
For Heaven is all around you
It's only 3 feet off your floor
And on the days you miss me so
Please know I'm at your side
I comfort you with my sweet touch
Your life, I help to guide
I leave you many loving signs
So you know I'm not far away
These signs are your reminders
That I'm in your life to stay

Some day our paths will meet again
When your sweet soul has flown
For now I'm there in all you do
For you are not alone

For I'll Always Be Your Loving Son

Please don't think that I'm gone, I'm in heaven
And my life here has only begun
Please just smile when you think of my memory
For I'll always be your loving son
Please look back on the times that you taught me
What I need in this life to succeed
I know sometimes that I was a challenge
But you taught me don't follow just lead
And I know that my life wasn't perfect
I took life by the horns without fear
Please know now that I'm perfect in heaven
I still love you mom and I'm right here
I'll be here wrapping my soul around you
When you feel that you're missing my touch
I'm right here drying tears upon your cheeks
Please just know that I love you so much
And when you think you're living without me
When you feel that you're losing your way
I'll be here shining light upon your path
Follow me Mom, I'll show you the way
And some day when you meet me in Heaven
And your tears you will no longer cry
You won't wonder if I am ok Mom
You will finally stop asking God why
You'll see then that I'm perfect in heaven
But for now please just trust what I say
Live your life to its fullest potential
Make me proud, try to smile each day
For the legacy that I have left you
Was not meant to be sadness and tears
Please just smile now when you think of me Mom
And let go of your sadness and fears

I'll send signs as I watch you from heaven
Little things that remind you of me
So have faith that we will be together
For together again mom we'll be

In Dreams

In Dreams I don't know heart ache
In Dreams I know no Fear
In Dreams I feel that you're alive
It's as if you're still right here
In Dreams I feel your gentle touch
In Dreams I see your Smile
In Dreams I hold you in my arms
If only for a while
In Dreams you try to calm me
In Dreams you say It's okay
In Dreams I have you at my side
As if you never went away
In Dreams I know you're Happy
In Dreams we both can fly
In Dreams I do not Miss you
I don't even ask God Why
In Dreams I know how close you are
In Dreams I see my best friend
In Dreams I know that I must go
Until I Dream Again.......

I Feel You Wrapped Inside My Soul

As the stars shine down upon me
In the darkness of the night
I look up and hope to see you
As you live in Heaven's light
They say that you can see me
And that heaven's all around
Do you know how much I love you
I hope you don't see when I've frowned
I wear your love upon my Heart
I feel you wrapped inside my soul
Memories of you, they make me smile
You're still the half that makes me whole
And when I wake to find each day
That you're no longer here with me
I hope you hear me speak your name
I'll carry on your legacy
So as you watch me from in Heaven
You're always welcome at my side
I hope to feel you standing with me
I hope I fill your soul with pride
And as I journey through this life
Until my life is also through
Please know I'm loving you from here
Until again I am with you

So Go On Now To Heaven

So go on now to Heaven
For your work on Earth is through
You have traveled your life's path
Your beautiful life you will review
You will see all of the times in life
You helped others along the way
You will know how much we loved you
And how we still love you today
You'll be proud of all the times
You put a smile inside our heart
We will still feel you at our side
As if we've never been apart
So go on now to Heaven
To live your life in God's pure love
Please send us signs when we do stumble
As you watch over from above
Please know that as we walk through life
That our sweet Souls are intertwined
Without the other incomplete
No Greater love than ours you'll find
So Go on now to Heaven
For someday when our life is done
We will meet you up in Heaven
Where our sweet soul's will then be One

Have You Ever Seen An Angel

Have you ever seen an Angel
Spread their wings and take to flight
Have you heard The Angel's Choir
Sing Amazing Grace and Silent Night
Have you felt the warmth of stars
As they light up the whole sky
Have you felt the Hand of Jesus
As he touches you and I
Have you ever felt white light
As it fills your soul with Love
Have you been free from all your pain
Or flown on wings of a white dove
You really needn't worry
About where I am today
For I am up in Heaven
Though I'm never far away
I try to send you comfort
For I know you miss me bad
In Heaven We're all happy
Please try not to be so sad
You still have lots of living
Your lessons are not through
Just know that as you live your life
That I still live through you
So do your very best
To put a smile upon your face
For I'm watching you from Heaven
This is such a Beautiful Place
And when your time is through
I shall be waiting at your side
I'll introduce you to the Angels
I'll be your Heavenly Guide

I'm Always With You

Do you feel me at your side
When you scream you miss me so
Do you know that I'm right next to you
Wiping your tears that seem to flow
I do listen when you tell me
How much you love me every day
I'm right here watching from Heaven
I truly never went away
I can see you carry guilt for me
That isn't yours to bare
Please know I would have lived forever
If I lived purely off your care
Let go of guilt and pain and anger
For it isn't serving you
Hold on to Memories of my love
They will be sure to see you through
Go out and live life to its fullest
For I'll be standing at your side
Oh how I love to see you smile
I'll be so proud that you sure tried
Please know that I completely love you
And I know that you love me too
My body couldn't live forever
My time on Earth was truly through
But I am on another journey
Of this Eternal live we live
For there is never end to our life
My Soul has so much more to give
So for now know that you still live
For you have learning yet to do
Please think of me right at your side
And know that I'm always with you

Happy Holidays To You On The Wings Of An Angel

The Holidays are coming
So what do we do
How do we celebrate
Here Without you
Now that you're in Heaven
How do we go on
It's just not the same here
Since the day you were gone
But wait just a minute
I just now recalled
All the sweet memories
In my life you installed
You taught me to love
And to share love the same
Your life was amazing
Your legacy is your fame
It is my job to share
The Traditions you made
And I'll share them for you
Our sweet memories won't fade
I will honor your life
Set your place at the table
Fill the children
With stories of you if I'm able
I will tell of your life
How you made my heart smile
How I'm Thankful I had You
If only for a while
So I'm sending a big
Happy Holidays to You
On the Wings Of an Angel
With a Kiss of Love Too

If Heaven Had A Stairway

If Heaven had a stairway
So that you could come see me
You would see that I am Happy
I am well, I'm fine, I'm free
If you could peek right into Heaven
You would see God's perfect love
You would feel that love surround you
As it does Me in Heaven Above
If there was a door to Heaven
That you could open once each day
You would see that I am right here
I never truly went away
If Heaven had a window
That you could stand at and look in
You would see a place of Beauty
And I would look at you and grin
I know your Faith has been a challenge
I know you find it hard to smile
I know you cry each night in your bed
I know I made your life worthwhile
But I ask you to just do one thing
Please carry me in all you do
My Soul is intertwined with your soul
And now my Soul, it lives through you

I Stopped To Think Of You Today

I stopped to think of you today
And pictured your sweet face
Your eyes how they would smile at me
Your sweet loving embrace
I stopped to think of you today
And how I miss you so
I cherish all the time we had before you had to go
I stopped to think of you today
I held your picture in my hand
It is so hard without you here with me
But I know you understand
I stopped to think of you today
I felt you standing next to me
I could feel your love right at my side
Oh how I'd surely love to see
I stopped to think of you today
And how you make my life complete
Sometimes I feel as though I'm missing half
Without you my heart skips a beat
I stopped to think of you today
And how I want to make you proud
I hope you see the way I honor you
I say my love for you out loud
I stopped to think of you today
I know you're perfect now above
And we will be together in Heaven again
Where we will share eternal love

As I Walked Through Heaven's Gates

As I walked through Heaven's Gates
I heard you ask me to please stay
If you could only see the beauty here
Please know that I'm not far away
There is no pain up here in Heaven
Anger and fear just disappear
I'm filled with Peace and Love each day
Now I watch over you from here
My journey there in life was through
But my pure spirit is so bright
I've graduated to the next phase
Eternal life in Gods Pure Light
And on the days that you must cry
Please know I'm standing at your side
I wipe your tears with my sweet love
You see, I never truly Died
So live your life now and be happy
Please Honor me in all you do
And someday this will all make sense
When I am here to welcome you

From Heaven My Dreams Will Be Blessed

As my head lies upon a pillow
And my body starts its rest
My Soul knows, soon you'll be at my side
From Heaven my dreams will be blessed
In life I long to hear your voice
I miss your warm loving embrace
I want to touch you with my hands
If only I could see your face
But in my dreams I have you with me
You walk beside me as we speak
I hear your voice as I remember it
And feel your kiss upon my cheek
You tell me that you're doing great
And not to worry since you've gone
You say you're with me as I live
You say you see me carry on
And when I wake up in the morning
And I don't have you at my side
I know you're watching me from Heaven
I know your Soul is filled with Pride
And although your life here is through
You know how hard it was to live
You said I have learning to do
My soul has so much more to give
And So I'll carry you with me
No matter how hard life may seem
For I know when I go to sleep
That I will see you in my dreams

And Now That You're In Heaven, I Will Share Your Legacy

You always made me smile
As you shared your life with me
And now that you're in Heaven
I will share your Legacy
I'll tell them of your loving eyes
And how you made me laugh
They'll hear my favorite memories
I'll speak on your behalf
You touched my life in many ways
And now it seems so clear
My life was blessed and changed by you
It seems as if you're here
I'll carry you in all I do
Through me you will live on
You'll share in my adventures
I'll live as if you are not gone
The traditions that we made in life
I will be sure to share
And I will keep your soul alive
For our Souls are now a pair
Then someday I will join you
Within God's light up above
And we will live for an Eternity
As we share Eternal Love

FARA GIBSON

You Try To Be The Strongest, It's Not Easy Being A Man

You hold our family tight
You do the very best you can
You try to be the strongest
It's not easy being a man
I see the tears inside of you
Your heart broken in two
Just know that I'm in Heaven
And I'm watching over you
I'm proud of all the ways
That you dry our family's tears
You tell them it's okay
As you work through your own fears
The way you hold them in your arms
Your tears, you never let them show
And as You put on a strong face
Your grief is more than they will know
I know it's hard to picture Heaven
It's tough to believe what you can't see
But, I am always all around you
I hear when you quietly talk to me
So Hold our family in your arms
And keep your chin up when you're sad
For I'm counting you your strength
To pull them through the good and bad
And someday when you get to Heaven
I will hold you close to me
And I will Thank You for being strong
For them when I just couldn't be

To My Child From Your Parent In Heaven

Oh Sweet Child of Mine, Please don't be sad
Since I walk in Heaven's light
For it truly was my time to go
And I keep you in my sight
I gave you life's foundation
And my legacy shines clear
So don't forget to live for me
I haven't left you, I'm right here
I see you as you stumble
And sometimes you even fall
But, please know that I'm proud of you
I'll pick you up, help you stand tall
Remember all the things I said
To make you who you are today
And please live your life in honor of me
As if I never went away
For a Parents love, it has no end
It lasts for all Eternity
And I'll greet you here with open arms
Someday when you come home to me

On This day Is My Angelversary

On this day is my Angelversary
But it is not a day to cry
For I'm right here with you from Heaven
So please don't sit and ask God Why
Please take the memories that I left you
And share them with all those we love
You make me smile when you speak of me
As I watch over you from Above
You see the life I lived was not defined
By the day my Soul moved on
I left you love and smiles and memories
Hold on to those for I'm not gone
I'm standing right here at your side
I wipe your tears when you are sad
But today's my Angelversary
Let's celebrate the times we had
Please know I would have lived forever
If love from you could have saved me
But, It was just my time to go
Some day when you are here you'll see
Passing is truly just a Chapter
For our Eternally Bright Soul
I feel the love that you send to me
You are the Half that makes me whole
So please find time today to celebrate
The love I left behind for you
And as you celebrate my life
I'll be there celebrating too

To Mom From Your Son In Heaven

Mom Even though I am in Heaven
My new chapter in life has begun
And nothing could ever come between
The love of a Mother and Son
You carried me as a baby
The bond we have will never bend
You will always be my sweet Mother
You are my Guiding Light, My Best Friend
We created sweet memories in life
The love that you gave saw me through
And now I will love you from Heaven
It is my turn to watch over you
So don't think that you're living without me
For my Spirit is just at your side
I see that you cry tears in your sleep
Your sadness for me you can't hide
Perhaps I'll send frogs when you miss me
To remind you of your silly boy
Or maybe just one little critter
So I can see those tears turned into Joy
Oh, Please Mom know that I am right here
I am perfect in Heaven's sweet light
And some day when you come to Heaven
I will hug you with all of my Might

I Am Standing Right Beside You

I am standing right beside you
As I wipe away your tear
You see I never really left you
For Heaven truly is right here
I hear you asking God
Why on Earth I had to go
But, I'm still standing at your side
I love you more than you could know
Heaven is truly all around you
I am the wind within your hair
I am the sun upon your face
Yes I am truly everywhere
I am standing right beside you
As you stumble and you fall
I pick you up and dust you off
And then I help you to stand tall
I am the feather on the ground
When you've missed me so that day
I am the wings on birds in flight
To tell you I'm not far away
I am standing right beside you
As your path continues on
So please don't ever think I left you
For I was never truly gone

Underneath My Smile Are Your Memories Left Behind

I know you are in Heaven now
And how I miss you so
But thinking of you has a way
Of making my Soul Glow
You always found time every day
To be loving and kind
And underneath my smile
Are your memories left behind
I know you wouldn't want to see
Me crying all the time
So if the choice is up to me
You'll be sure to see me shine
I'll make you proud in all I do
And you can live through me
I'll reach my goals in life I planned
Oh just you wait and see
The Angels up in Heaven
May have to watch through one peeked hand
As I live life to its fullest
My Stumbles and falls, they may be Grande
But know that as I'm living
I have learning yet to do
And someday when my time is done
I'll be in Heaven with You

FARA GIBSON

I'm Watching Over You From Heaven

I'm watching over you from Heaven
I'll be your strength when you are weak
I'll be the rock that you may lean on
When your tears fall upon your cheek
Please know that I am proud of you
For trying hard to carry on
I know without me there its hard
But know my spirit is not gone
I see the way you honor my life
In little things that you still do
Please know that as you honor me
That I am always there with you
I hear you speak to me each day
I see your smiles and your tears
Please know I'm perfect now in Heaven
I hope that helps to ease your fears
God says you still have life to live
Please know that I am at your side
And as you sometimes find life hard
You make my soul shine with pure pride
For you are living life to grow
And oh the growing you have done
Then someday you'll be here in Heaven
Where our two souls will be then be one

For As My Angel Watches Over Me

I have an Angel up in Heaven
And that sweet Angel has a Name
My Angel watches me as I live
Life here without them isn't the same
As they watch down on me from Heaven
I wonder what it is they see
Do they see me as I cry for them
If so, I don't want that to be
I hope that they can see me Happy
I hope to always make them proud
I will just show them that I love them
I'd shout it out amongst a crowd
I'll carry them each day that I live
They'll have a space inside my Heart
I'll honor them in all that I do
As if we've never been apart
For as my Angel watches over me
I know they wouldn't want my tears
They don't want guilt or pain or anger
They filled my life with love for years
So as I journey now in my life
I know their always at my side
They lift me up the days I stumble
They're proud of me because I tried
And some day I will be an Angel
And we will meet again above
For now they'll live their life through my eyes

FARA GIBSON

Please Know I Never Really Left You

Please know I never really left you
Although my journey there was through
For I am home now up in Heaven
Where I am watching over you
I know you think you live without me
But I am right here at your side
Though you can't hold me in your arms
Please know my spirit never died
I have asked God to send you comfort
For I don't want to see you cry
There is so much more we will share
You need not keep asking God Why
Our Spirit's Journeys are Eternal
And this was just me passing through
Onto the next part of my journey
Where someday you will travel too
So for now, know that I do love you
And I know that you love me too
And someday we will meet in Heaven
When your sweet Journey there is Through
For now I'll live my life through your eyes
So honor me in all you do
And someday this will all make sense
When your journey there is through

Our Souls Are One, They're Intertwined

There is no thought I have without you
Since you have grown your Angel Wings
I feel your spirit all round me
A light in my soul your love brings
For you I keep within my heart
The memories you have left behind
Your life has blessed my path with love
Our Souls are one, they're intertwined
I see the signs you send from Heaven
They make me smile and think of you
You are Eternal now at God's Side
For Spirit's lives are never through
Your Beauty I'll always hold on to
You've left a twinkle in my eye
I'll share your legacy with others
For you I'll keep my head held high
For someday we will meet in Heaven
And I know you'll be waiting there
To take my Hand and say I love you
And once again we'll be a pair

I'm Watching You From Heaven

I'm watching you from Heaven
And I see you're crying tears
You know a smile is all I ask of you
Please remember all my years
I'm watching you from heaven
From a place of pure sweet love
There is no reason to forgive you
There is no sorrow up above
I'm watching you from Heaven
Please let go of guilt and pain
It is not serving you to carry it
It will hold you back from gain
I'm watching you from Heaven
As you try to carry on
Please know I am at your side
For my spirit is not gone
I'm watching you from Heaven
As I leave you signs each day
Heaven's 3 feet off your floor
I am never far away
I'm watching you from Heaven
Someday our paths will cross again
For now please enjoy your journey
My Life, my love, and my best friend

Please Hold On To All My Love

Please hold on to all my love
The memories that I left for you
The times we shared a laugh and smile
Those times will surely see you through
And please let go of pain and heartache
Let go of all that holds you down
I want to lift you up with my love
For I don't want to see you frown
Life here in Heaven is just perfect
So please don't worry about me
I'm filled with pure sweet love from God
It's Beautiful here, some day you'll see
The legacy I left behind
Has surely changed your world I know
Your tears for me, they come from love
And through those tears, your soul does grow
You see I left for you a gift
When I passed, then you did receive
I blessed you with amazing strength
That you would find as you would grieve
Please know I'm proud of all you do
I watch you with a loving smile
We sure are blessed for time we had
If only for a little while
Oh, don't you worry, I'll be here
And surely more time we will share
Yes here in Heaven we're Eternal
I will watch over you with care
Someday your life there will be through
And I'll be standing at your side
So for now hold on to my love
As you enjoy your life's sweet ride

FARA GIBSON

You Were Not Meant To Save Me

You were not meant to save me
I wasn't meant to stay
So please stop blaming yourself
Since I have gone away
My time on Earth was over
There's something you should know
My soul had reached its Growth there
It was my time to go
Don't cry for all the Could Have's
The What If's and If Only
Let go of all the guilt you hold
Then you won't feel so lonely
I Graduated life there
And into Heaven's light
I live within God's peace here
My soul is perfectly Bright
Life there is but a chapter
Of a book that carries on
I'm just on the next page now
I really am not gone
The Angels up in Heaven
Help me watch you as you live
Your life there isn't over yet
You have so much to give
Your life there will touch others
Just as my life there touched you
So be sure to touch them softly
And place love within their view
Just know this will make sense someday
We will look back and smile
You are just merely passing through

We only stay there for a while
So please hold on to my love
As you walk through life each day
And know that I am right here
And Right here, I'll always stay

FARA GIBSON

I'm Flying High Now With The Angels

I'm flying high now with the angels
I soar now in God's perfect light
Please picture me as perfect now
As my soul has taken to flight
You need not wonder if I'm happy
My soul shines now with perfect love
There is no sadness, pain, or anger
As I live in Heaven above
You know those prayers you say to me
As you are lying in your bed
I hear them all, yes I still hear you
Even when you speak in your head
And when I hear you speak my name
It fills my soul with love and pride
You think you live life now without me
But, I am right here at your side
Chase all the dreams you can in life
And as you catch them wear your crown
I'll cheer you on from Heaven's arms
And Pick you up if you fall down
Just know I'm loving you from here
I sure am proud of all you do
And someday when you get to Heaven
I will be waiting here for you

9

A Letter From Heaven

Dear..........,

Now that I am in Heaven, I know that life for you there just isn't the same. I want you to know that I hear you say how much you miss me and love me every day. Yes, I still hear your words and your thoughts to me. I love you so much too. My love for you will never waiver from Heaven. I can't say that I miss you because you see, missing you is a negative emotion and we simply don't have negative emotions here in Heaven. And so, instead of missing you for all of the years that you have left in your life, I will Love you through them instead. I know it is hard to continue on when you feel you are walking through life without me, but I want you to know that I am right here next to you. I walk through your life with you now, guiding you and helping you along the way. Our relationship never ended when I graduated to Heaven, it is simply different now. Heaven is all around you. Heaven is truly only 3 feet off of your floor. I want you to look for the signs that I leave for you from Heaven. You won't have to look very hard because since Heave surrounds you, I will surround you with signs in so many different ways. You see, I am limitless when it comes to leaving you signs. Birds, butterflies, silly shaped rocks, rainbows, clouds that look like me, electronic mishaps, songs on your radio, coins, feathers, oh I wouldn't begin to be able to tell you how many different kinds of signs that I can bring into your path. When you see the signs I send, don't let your conscious mind tell you that it wasn't from me, because it really was. Sometimes you may miss the signs that I send you because it is hard to see the beauty in the world around you through tears and that is okay, I will just keep sending signs of love until those tears clear. I am not missing out on your milestones or the milestones within our family. When babies are born into our family since my passing, I get to hold them first here in Heaven. When wedding days come, I walk the bride down the aisle. I am at graduations and Birthdays and Anniversary celebrations. I love the way you think of me so often. I think the ways that you and the family have honored me since I journeyed home to Heaven are pretty amazing. Please try not to dwell on the day and way that I passed each day, for my legacy of love that I left behind for you is so much more beautiful than my passing. It hurts you to think of my passing and that hurt is not the best part of me that I left for you. I want you to hold on to our sweet memories that we share with one another. When you find yourself in a day of tears, please just replace one of those tears with your favorite memory of me. I will sit with you as you remember me and enjoy the memory with you. I know you would love to see me in dreams every night as you go to sleep. I would love to be there in your dreams each night as well. When you say out loud, "I never see you in my dreams", it places blocks in my way because your energy says that you don't see me. I want to help you with that. I want you to change that phrase to, " I look forward to seeing you in my dreams in your perfect timing". It will help you to place this positive focus on seeing me in your dreams when the timing is right. The reason I don't come every night in your dreams is because you really do need space to work through your grief as well. You see, you are gaining more strength through your grief than you ever knew you could carry in life. Part of that strength is my gift to you and that gift will only make sense someday when you return home to Heaven here with me. We spend our lives there living for our spiritual growth. Some of the most beautiful and strong spirits write some of the most difficult paths and I want you to be so proud of yourself for the life you are living with all of the obstacles you placed within your path. I also want you to know how extremely proud of you I am as I watch you learn and grow from Heaven. God didn't punish you when I went to Heaven before you. I simply reached my soul's beautiful goal of growth in life. I reached that amazing goal before you and it didn't mean that I left you for one moment. I graduated to the next part of my eternal journey in Heaven. Oh, you should have seen it when I got here!! All of our family and friends who graduated to Heaven before me were right at my side to greet me when I arrived! Even the pets that we had long the way were waiting with smiles and wags as I walked into Heaven's light! I went into a review of my life after I arrived and it was truly amazing to see all of the lives I touched there with mine. I got to re-live my life through the eyes of each and every person that my life touched along the way. It was beautiful to watch my life through your eyes as well. Don't worry, when you get here, you will get to review your life through everyone's eyes as well as your own and even through mine. There will be moments you are extremely proud of and there will also be moments that you will recognize that you could have handled differently. But, the beauty of those moments is that you are living and in your life, not everything will be perfect and that is just part of our growth. None of us can take back the things we could have done differently, but we sure can grow from those moments. Of course, me telling you this now gives you an opportunity to look at the days in your future differently so that you will be proud of them when you look back. I didn't have to make myself a home when I arrived to Heaven because I already had one. You see, I lived in Heaven before I lived there on Earth with you and I simply returned to my beautiful home in Heaven. You will remember it too when you get here. The colors here in Heaven aren't like anything you have there on Earth! The light that fills the air lifts our souls with love for it is made of God. The Angel's choir has such a Heavenly sound that it brings peaceful showers of love down upon you all on Earth. The weather here is perfect always. Time doesn't exist here which is really nice too, I mean we don't have to run around heaven looking at our watches on our spirit wrists worried about being late for anything ha ha. You see, you can't place a time on Eternity. We don't work here in Heaven the way that you all work there on Earth, but we do work. We work on our spiritual growth as we are part of God and we are always working on the beautiful evolution of our Souls growth and strength. Just remember as you walk through your life each and every day, that I am right here at your side. I cheer you on in your times of Greatness and I wipe your tears in your moments of pain. So what if you have a day of tears, I will stay at your side for comfort. I can tell you that I am most proud of you as you get out and live life to its fullest. I don't want you to think that you can no longer live because I am "Gone" because I am not gone at all. Carry me with you in all that you do for I am here. The dreams that you wish you could have lived out with me in life are still possible and don't you worry, I won't miss them. My biggest message of all in this letter from Heaven to you is that I am perfect, don't worry about me, I Love you, and I am with you for always, I want to see you live life to its fullest, I want to see you catch your dreams and I see you and hear you always both when you speak out loud and even when you speak silently to me in your mind. Someday this will all make perfect sense when you get to Heaven with me so don't worry that it doesn't make sense now. Just know that you are a miracle because you are made of God and because you are a miracle, you are capable of creating miracles as well. I Love You......

All Of My Love,
Me Up In Heaven

Made in the USA
Las Vegas, NV
07 November 2023